National Spinal Cord Injury
Association
6701 Democracy Blvd., Ste. 300-9
Bethesda, Maryland 20817

DS Medical

Helping you
make a
difference

Athletes come in all shapes and sizes and
DS Medical is there to support your athletic
endeavors through sponsorships such as:

- PossAbilities
- The American Association of
  AdaptedSports™ Programs, Inc.
- Moving Mountains

today and tomorrow!

Photos Courtesy of The American
Association of AdaptedSports™ Programs

Here's a fun challenge for your enjoyment.
Unscramble the letters that spell things you enjoy.

1) A R C G I N _____
2) C S O R C E _____
3) N E T S I N _____
4) U B Y G R _____
5) O E K Y C H _____

6) F N U _____
7) K E L A B S T L B A _____
8) I G N K S I _____
9) G I S F N I H _____
10) S A G E M _____

1) racing 2) soccer 3) tennis 4) rugby 5) hockey 6) fun 7) basketball 8) skiing 9) fishing 10) games

DS MEDICAL
Bringing Healthcare Solutions Home

MKW4

1-888-SCI-HELP
(724-4357)
www.dsmedical.com

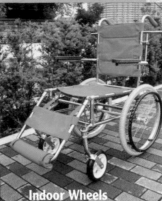

Hey Kids!
We've got the
Chair for you

The Invacare® Top End® Terminator™ Jr. is a chair for kids and is built to grow as you get bigger. It comes in lots of cool colors too, like Sunny Yellow, Denim Blue, Jewel Green, Purple, Red and more. Ask mom or dad to visit Invacare's website at www.invacare.com for more information.

The Terminator Jr. is a pediatric chair built with optimum wheel position for maximum mobility. With adjustable seat depth and center of gravity, and a choice of 18, 20, 22 or 24-inch spoke or composite wheels, it is a perfect fit for kids.

Yes, you can.™

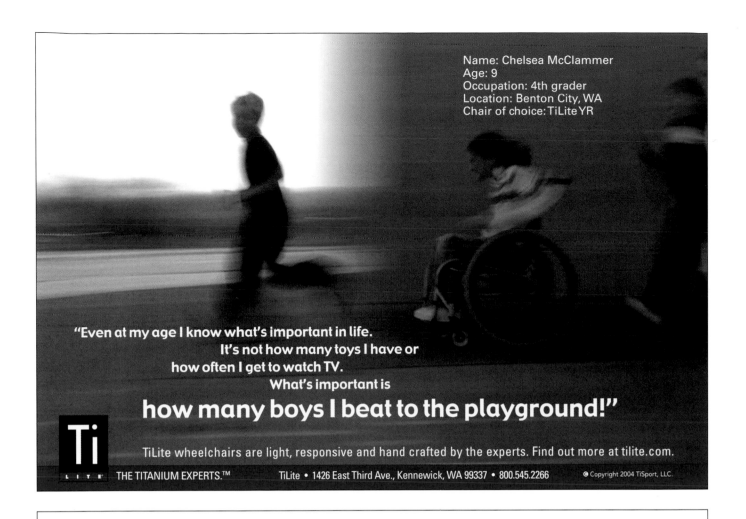

Would you like to see a MAGAZINE called Kids on Wheels?

Visit us on the Web at
www.kidsonwheels.us
and let us know what you think!

Kids
on
Wheels

A Young Person's Guide to Wheelchair Lifestyle

Kids on Wheels is designed to provide accurate information in regard to the subject matter covered. The publisher is not responsible for errors, ommisions or changes in fact.

Kids on Wheels is sold with the understanding that the publisher is not liable for personal injury or property damage resulting from any of the activities or products described within.

Cover photo credits, top to bottom:
Susan Collins, Lynne Jaffe, P. Sue Kullen, Adaptive Adventures

Distributed by Leonard Media Group
P.O. Box 220
Horsham, PA
19044
888-850-0344, ext. 209

Web site: www.kidsonwheels.us

Library of Congress Control Number: 2004107738

ISBN 0-9712842-3-7

Printed in the United States of America

Kids
on
Wheels

A Young Person's Guide to Wheelchair Lifestyle

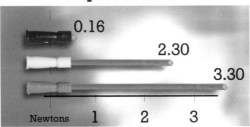

table of contents

Table of contents continued after next page

Photo courtesy of Pride Mobility

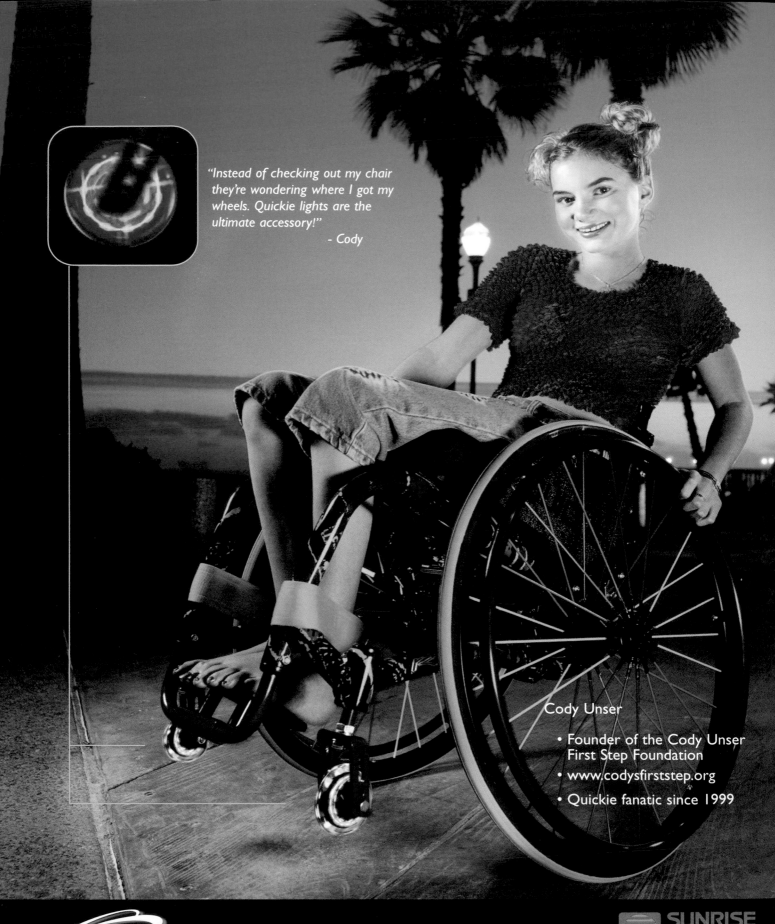

"Instead of checking out my chair they're wondering where I got my wheels. Quickie lights are the ultimate accessory!"

- Cody

Cody Unser

- Founder of the Cody Unser First Step Foundation
- www.codysfirststep.org
- Quickie fanatic since 1999

table of contents

(Continued)

Photo courtesy of Landscape Structures

What's This Book About?

This book is about kids on wheels living a full life. A life full of fun, friends, family, animals and nature. A life full of sports, art, learning and success. A life full of choices.

It can be about your life.

In these pages, you will meet active kids like you who are using adaptive equipment and other resources to get the most out of life. You will also find lots of Web sites and phone numbers that can lead you to more information. Use them. Sometimes it takes work to have fun, but it's worth it. You can take responsibility for making your life the way you want it. Ask questions, think big, follow your dreams.

It's your life. Live it!

A Word About Independence

All kids need their families to give them food, clothes and a safe home so they can grow into healthy adults. So everyone — whether living with a disability or not — starts out dependent.

In a way, it is every kid's "job" to grow more and more independent, so that when the time comes to move away from your parents, you'll be able to live on your own with confidence. This job may be harder for kids with disabilities. But this book is written from the point of view that *independence is the most important goal you can have.*

So what does independence really mean? It doesn't mean that you have to do everything for yourself. It does mean doing the things you can do without hurting yourself. Most importantly, it means knowing what you need or want. It means making choices and decisions to build the life you want. And it means knowing when to ask for help.

Asking for help may not sound like independence, but there is a way to do it that allows you to be in control of your own life. This takes practice, but one day it will feel natural if you respect yourself and others.

People who learn all these skills of independent living are said to be "empowered." If you break down that word, you can see that it means you have the *power* to direct your life. That is independence. It is a goal worth striving for, and it is within your reach.

Devin Keppel-Brown: Enjoying Life

If you look up *vivacious* in the dictionary, it says: "spirited, lively, bubbly, full of life." It might as well say "Devin Keppel-Brown."

Devin is 8 years old, and in third grade at Weston School in Manchester, New Hampshire. A few days before his third birthday, Devin was hit by a car while crossing the street.

In the accident, Devin's spinal cord was injured at the C1-2 level, which means he can't move any part of his body below his neck. Devin uses a motorized, "sip and puff" wheelchair that he controls with his mouth. He breathes with the help of a ventilator.

That's the disability. And then there's Devin.

Devin has gone horseback riding, canoeing, tubing, swimming, fishing and hiking. He has traveled all over the eastern United States with his mom in their accessible van, including 11 days at Disney World. Devin went on every ride. "My favorite was Thunder Mountain," he says. "It went so fast, my eyes were bugged out of my head!"

Fast is Devin's favorite way to travel, whether it's in a speedboat, a roller coaster, or his chair cranked up to seventh gear. He'll do 360s in a parking lot, or zoom down the hall in school (but only in third gear).

Devin really wants to go jet-skiing.

"Keep trying until you do what you want. When it's hard, keep trying even harder."

His mom hasn't figured that one out yet — ventilators and water are not a good match. But they haven't ruled it out. Devin's mom says, "If there's something he wants to do, we usually find a way."

Devin's parents both ride motorcycles, and they designed a special sidecar for Devin. "Once they get it made, we'll all ride together," says Devin. "The wind will blow in my face, it will be like flying!"

Most of us don't get to choose our parents, but when Devin's mom married Adam Strobridge, Devin asked Adam to be his dad. "Let's see, Adam or my other dad?" asks Devin. "Does my other dad play with me? Nope! Does he help me with my homework? No! Do I go anywhere with him? No! Adam — does he play with me? Yes! Does he help me with my homework? Yes! Does he do fun stuff with me? Yes! Do we go places together? Yes! So Adam is my dad now. He earned it. No contest."

Devin gets good grades, especially in math. He has lots of friends, but sometimes the kids in school get on his nerves. "In my class, no one listens to the teacher. The teacher always has to yell at them, and then they *still* don't do the lesson. And it's like that every day!"

You might get the impression that Devin is more mature than the rest of his class. This is a rumor he hotly denies. "Me, mature? Yeah, right. I am NOT mature, I am not!" To prove his point, Devin says, "My favorite show is Power Rangers.

Resource

Champ Camp
P.O. Box 40407
Indianapolis, IN 46240
317-415-5530
admin@champcamp.org

I'm 8 years old and I still watch it! *And* I use a nightlight! I'm afraid of the dark! Does that sound mature to you?"

Every year, Devin goes to Champ Camp, a one-week camp for kids who have tracheostomies or use ventilators. They go fishing, horseback riding, canoeing, hiking, and in general never stop moving.

Devin was the only Champ Camper who had a spinal cord injury. At first he found it strange to be around a lot of kids who had disabilities. But Devin made great friends at camp that he looks forward to seeing every year.

Camp was also the first time Devin had ever been away from his mom. She thinks Devin grew up a lot that week — an accusation he denies.

There are only 10 other kids in the United States who have the same kind of injury as Devin. There aren't many adults, either — actor Christopher Reeve is one of the few. To everyone, no matter how old they are or what differences they have, Devin says, "Don't give up. Keep trying until you do what you want. When it's hard, keep trying even harder."

—*By Laura Kaminker*

Kayla Wheeler: Doing It Her Way

Seven-year-old Kayla Wheeler doesn't use the word "can't." When someone tells her she can't do something, that just makes her work harder to figure out a way she *can* do it.

One time at a carnival, she really wanted to play the game where you throw darts to pop balloons. Her left elbow doesn't bend and she has only three fingers on that hand so her parents weren't sure she could aim the dart or throw it far enough. They bought her some darts anyway though, and sure enough, she

popped three balloons right away. Then she spun around with her hand on her hip and said, "Never underestimate the power of Kayla Marie Wheeler." Her mom says, "I guess she told me!"

Her mom also tried to talk her out of going to a cheerleading workshop led by high school girls. She told Kayla, "They will be doing a lot of things that you can't do." Kayla replied, "I don't care, I'll do it my own way." And she did: She went to the workshop, learned her own routine, and then joined the other girls who cheered for the high school basket-

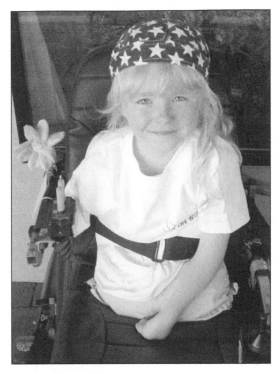

"Make sure if people are teasing you that you don't tease them back. Just say, 'That wasn't that nice,' and go find your friends and play with them."

ball team that weekend.

The next time Kayla wanted to try something new, her mom didn't say that dreaded "can't" word. She just watched proudly as Kayla passed a swim test at a local pool and announced that now she wanted to go off the diving board. Her mom says, "Next thing I know, I look up and there's my tiny girl up on the high dive! She dove off and couldn't wait to do it again!"

Kayla takes her fearless attitude into everything she does, which includes skiing and other outdoor adventures like riding ATVs with her family. She especially likes camping and other activities with her Brownie troop. She has 25 Brownie patches. "I like the 'Manners' one," she says.

Studying for the manners badge helped her learn to deal with people who stare at her in public, but her mom says she has always been good at talking to people. "It's my job," Kayla told her mom when she was just 2 years old.

She's even polite to kids who are mean. Her advice is: "Make sure if peo-

ple are teasing you that you don't tease them back. Just say, 'That wasn't that nice,' and go find your friends and play with them."

Skiing is Kayla's newest love. "It was something I thought I couldn't do until my mom told me there's a special ski I could use." Now she's had six lessons on a bi-ski. "I was scared to ski, but I did it anyway," Kayla says. Kayla lives in Washington State, where there are some great mountains for skiing.

When she's not trying a new activity, Kayla is playing at home with her friends, her parents or little brother, Sam.

Kayla also likes school, where she says her disability gives her an advantage on Field Day. "Since I have no legs, I always win the Limbo at Field Day. When the other kids have to bend a little, I just go right under the stick!"

If she's not scooting around on the ground or on her skateboard, Kayla uses a very cool power wheelchair. It can lower her to the ground for things like gardening — and lift her up for stuff like fishing or selling Girl Scout cookies (she sold 319 boxes this year!).

So what's the next new thing for Kayla? She wants to take a dance class. Her mom thought about saying "you can't," but before she could, Kayla said, "I'll do it my own way."
— *By Jean Dobbs*

Caitlin McDermott: Team Player

Caitlin McDermott is a 10-year-old sports fan! Born with spina bifida, Caitlin fell in love with wheelchair basketball at 9 years old. She plays with Adaptive Sports & Adventure Programs, or ASAP in Charlotte, North Carolina.

"It's just really competitive and it brings out my positive spirit in doing teamwork," she says. "Everyone who knows me, knows when we're in defense, I defend the basket."

A few summers ago, she learned to swim independently. "Swimming was harder at first than I thought it would be because I didn't feel my legs in the water or have my legs to propel," she recalls. "But when I felt more comfortable in the water, it was really cool." Last summer she tried water skiing and plans to do more.

Another sport she likes is track and field. "In field, I basically throw things like a softball, a club that you flick out and a shot put — a ball that's harder than a baseball," she explains. She also enjoys wheelchair racing and her parents are trying to get her a lighter wheelchair made out of titanium.

"I like winning," she says, explaining her love of sports. "I don't get discouraged when we lose, though. To me, it's all about playing the game and having fun." And making friends too. Through wheelchair basketball, she became friends with another girl who uses a chair and likes basketball as much as Caitlin. They recently had a sleep over, their first with another wheelchair user.

"We have a lot in common," Caitlin says of her new friend. "Other kids not in wheelchairs can do lots of things, like go up curbs. We have to move together and we stay at the same speed."

Caitlin dreams of being a veterinarian because she loves animals. "My whole room is filled with stuffed animals," she says. "I walk my friend Lauren's dog too, like it's my own." When she was younger, she had a dog named Daisy. Now she's applying for a Canine Companion. "I basically just want help to move around the house, help with my book bag. Sometimes I'm rushed in the morning and feel really tired and about to give up," she explains. "So it would be nice to have a dog to help me."

From early on, Caitlin liked moving. When she was 1 year old, her father made her a "rolling chair" out of an infant's booster seat and a wheeled tray, the kind you put trash cans on. The back had a big handle, and the sides had big wheels she could push herself, tiny as she was. Though she can now use forearm crutches and has spotty sensation down to her knees, Caitlin's main form of mobility is her wheelchair.

She doesn't think it's that big of a deal and advises other kids to not look at using a wheelchair as being different. "I think of myself as a regular kid and I do almost everything other kids do."

— *By Kathe A. Conti*

Conway Thompson: Smiling Eagle Boy

When Conway Thompson saw other youngsters performing traditional Native American dance at a powwow, he wanted to join in. "I saw the other kids dancing and it looked like fun," Conway says. "I told my mom I'd like to try that."

Now 14, he has been dancing for three years and has earned 13 eagle feathers.

Conway, who lives in Timber Lake, South Dakota, was diagnosed with muscular dystrophy when he was 8 months old. He has used a wheelchair since he was a toddler, but he has never let his disability stop him from having fun, and his desire to dance was no different.

Conway dances in a division called "grass dance," and he wears colorful costumes with fringed pants, a headdress and traditional buckskin moccasins that his grandfather made for him.

Reaction to Conway's participation as a dancer has been very positive. "People all say I inspire them," he says.

The dance schedule can be hard, with powwows throughout the region during the summer, each lasting for three days. "You dance all three days of the powwow," Conway explains. "Sometimes, by the time we're done, I'm pretty tired."

When he's not dancing, Conway shares the interests of most 14-year-old boys. "When the weather's bad I like to play Nintendo," he says. "I have a hunting game that's my favorite." An eighth-grader at Timber Lake High School, he says computers are his favorite subject.

It is also clear that his Lakota heritage plays a very important role in his life. Even before he started dancing, Conway had been given a Lakota name by his grandfather that translates as

Photo courtesy of Pride Mobility

Smiling Eagle Boy. "His grandfather gave him that name because, in spite of his [disability], he's still a smiling kid and he smiles all the time," says his mom. While his Jazzy wheelchair does not have an official Lakota name, Conway says his choice would be War Pony.

—*Adapted from an article by Pride Mobility*

Elizabeth Hassler: Magic Sneezes and Winning Speeches

Talking on the phone with Elizabeth Hassler is fun, because she's funny and very smart. Elizabeth, a fifth grader with cerebral palsy, takes drama lessons and recently starred in her school play at Joaquin-Miller Elementary in Oakland, California. She doesn't think being the lead in her school play was a big deal, though. "I would hardly even call that acting — the

play wasn't that good," she says. "I mean, it was called *Magical Sneeze.*"

In the play she sat on stage and sneezed. Each time she sneezed something strange would happen, like one person would split into two people. Then she'd sneeze and they'd go back to one person again. "It was just kind of weird," she says.

OK, maybe she has a point there — the play was kind of weird.

But Elizabeth's acting skills impressed Liane Yasumoto, director of the Corporation on Disabilities and Telecommunication, so much that Liane is creating a new drama class for kids with and without disabilities. "Elizabeth is a burst of energy, and she makes me smile and laugh," says Liane, who also

uses a wheelchair. "She told me about some of the drama exercises she took and they're pretty advanced. Already having the lead in her play, that's something."

Besides acting, Elizabeth loves to write and she competed in her school's speechwriting contest, called the Martin Luther King Jr. Oratorical contest. Elizabeth made it to the semifinals with her speech modeled on Martin Luther King Jr.'s famous "I Have a Dream" speech.

Elizabeth has a light-hearted side, too. She likes to hang out with her friends and go to sleepovers. What else? "I like the Dixie Chicks and I'll admit to liking Madonna, even though it's silly, freaky," she says. "It's kind of old to like Madonna."

But like most creative people, Elizabeth keeps an open mind — whether about "old school" music or new artistic expressions. "I'm a Junior Girl Scout," she says, "and my mom is going to teach us how to draw still life with oil pastels."

Her open mind also helps her at school, which is in a city neighborhood, not the suburbs. Elizabeth's mom says, "I want my kids to be comfortable in a diverse world, and not automatically put up barriers to people who look different than them."

Elizabeth's winning speech shows she's taken that lesson to heart: "My dream is the day that people will no longer be afraid of their differences. It is the day that rumors are not believed and people are not taunted. ... My dream is peace — and I hope to see this dream realized in my lifetime."

—*By Josie Byzek*

Thomas Weigand-Watkinson: So Many Joys, So Little Time

Thomas Weigand-Watkinson likes to go fast. The faster the better, especially when he's racing — which is why his parents are trying to get a lighter wheelchair. "My old wheelchair is dark blue and heavy," Thomas explains. "So I can't go super fast, just a little fast."

Thomas is 7 years old and lives in Norwich, Connecticut. Born with spina bifida, he can stand with braces and walk a little bit with a walker, but mostly he uses a manual wheelchair. Thomas stays busy with a lot of hobbies.

He joined the Cub Scouts in 2002 and wants to go all the way to Eagle Scout. He has attended two "Camporees" (sort of Cub Scout pow wows) and this past summer went on his first overnight camping trip with his dad, the den leader. "I like being at the camps," he says. "Last camp, they had s'mores. That was my favorite part." He and his parents also appreciate the accessible campgrounds the Scouts maintain. While at camp, Thomas discovered a talent for BB gun shooting and archery.

Two years ago, Thomas started taking pottery classes. He likes pottery because he can easily fix a piece if it's not turning out the way he likes. He has made coil pots, bowls, candle holders and other items, some hand built and some thrown on the wheel. Among his favorite hand-built pieces are a swimming pool and a starfish. "I really like to glaze my pieces. It's like painting, and I love to paint." He also enjoys the chance to display his work at the studio's annual exhibit and talk to people about pottery.

For years Thomas has been riding Hope, the horse his Grandmother keeps on her farm. But recently, after a two-

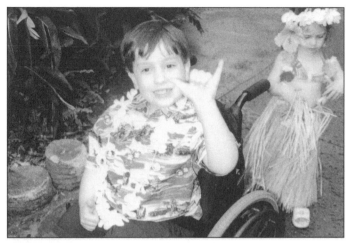

year wait, he was accepted into a therapeutic riding class and discovered the joys of trotting — going fast on a horse. Now he just has to convince his Grandmother to let him do that at the farm as well. "My favorite part was telling the horse to trot. Bouncy, bouncy, bouncy. It felt like I was on a trampoline," he says with a laugh.

In the summer of 2003, Thomas and his family attended the National Sports Disability Festival held at Connecticut College. When his sister said she'd had fun at the festival, Thomas said that he had *more* fun because he got to hang out with so many other kids in chairs. That was a new experience for him, and he was ready to sign up on the spot. So far he's been working on his basketball game and training in track racing for the Cruisers team, based about an hour away from his home.

When he's not busy with all his various activities, Thomas is home-schooled by his mom, who was a teacher before becoming a parent. And his biggest dream: to visit LegoLand in California some day. Preferably while using a speedy wheelchair.

— *By Kathe A. Conti*

Robbie Gordon: A Natural Talent

Robbie Gordon is a football fanatic. Robbie lives in St. Petersburg, Florida, which is right next to Tampa, so his favorite pro football team is the Tampa Bay Buccaneers, who won the Super Bowl in 2003. He met a couple of the players and even got their autographs.

But most of all, Robbie, who is 8, loves to play football from the manual wheelchair he uses because he has spina bifida.

"I just roll around and throw the ball, chase the ball, throw and catch, throw and catch," he says. "I love intercepting the ball." He plays football with his friends on the hardtop outside school so he has a firm surface for his wheelchair. Their team is called the Hot Shots. "I play right receiver and linebacker and safety and quarterback," he says. Sometimes tight end."

He also likes to play basketball in the gymnasium from his wheelchair, but not as much. "When I miss a shot, I get mad, and I hate getting mad," he says.

Photos courtesy of Invacare Top End

Robbie is in the third grade at Tyrone Elementary School. His favorite subjects are math because he loves to add and subtract, "especially the really big numbers," and social studies because he likes to learn about different places.

Robbie showed another natural talent — modeling — a couple of years ago when he posed for an ad for the Invacare Top End wheelchair company.

His sister, Valerria, who is 7 and in the second grade, also uses a wheelchair because of spina bifida. "Sometimes we have wheelchair races in the hallway at school," he says.

If you ask Robbie about Valerria, he mentions that they sometimes fight and he doesn't like it when she bothers him when he's playing a video game. But his mom says he sticks up for his sister. "He won't let anybody mess with her," she says. "He's very protective of her. They depend on each other for a lot of stuff and learn from each other."

Robbie also loves to sing at his church, Mount Zion Progressive Baptist Church, where he is in the choir and a mime group. His favorite song to sing is "If it had not been for the Lord on my side, what would I do?"

"It feels exciting and real great," to sing in front of the whole congregation, Robbie says. "Sometimes I feel a little scared when all the people are looking at me."

His mom says Robbie is a real natural at performing. "He's got a gift of making it happen in his own way," she says. "When he sings, 'The Lord is on my side,' he'll hold his hands up to heaven. He always gets a standing ovation."

—By Carolyn Said

Luke Stepter: 'Nothing I Can't Do'

Ask anyone in Kevil, Kentucky, and they'll all tell you the same thing — Luke Stepter is the kind of kid that other people want to be around. Even the kids at his school fight to see who gets to play with him at recess. "I'm just a pretty happy kid, I guess," says Luke. "I always have been."

Luke, 10, has cerebral palsy. He was born premature and weighed less than three pounds. Because his CP affects Luke's ability to control his arms and legs, he has never been able to walk. In order to get around, he controls his wheelchair by pressing his head against the headrest mounted on his chair. To go forward, he pushes his head straight back. If he wants to turn left or right, he simply moves his head in that direction while pressing against his headrest. Because of Luke's outgoing personality, he was recently chosen to appear in a series of magazine ads around the world for the Pride wheelchair company.

"When it first came out, I told everyone I was a movie star," laughs Luke. "They even have the picture hanging up in my school." So popular is Luke, that students at a nearby high school built wooden flaps that can be installed on the side of his wheelchair. At recess, he can often be found maneuvering around a field full of soccer players, using the flaps to help him guide a large ball into the soccer goal.

Luke's candy apple red wheelchair, which he received last year, has been a dream come true. "I used to get frustrated because it was so hard to go places in my old wheelchair," he says. "Now I can practically go anywhere I want without anyone's help. That makes me feel good."

When he's not tooling around in his wheelchair, his mom straps him onto the family's Honda four-wheeler and heads off through the countryside. "We use a weightlifting belt for a harness and we ride around through the woods and mud puddles," he laughs. "My sister rides on the back." In the winter, he gets towed through the snow on a sled. When the weather warms up, he loves putting on a lifejacket and just floating in the water at a public pool near his house.

Luke truly believes his future is limitless. "When I grow up, I want to be a police officer," he says. "I know I'll never walk, but my mom always tells me there's nothing I can't do if I put my mind to it, and I know she's right."

—By Ed Oldham

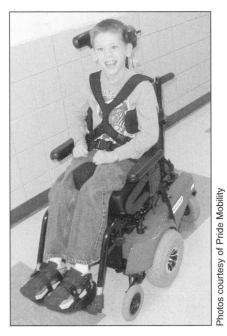

Photos courtesy of Pride Mobility

"When the ad first came out, I told everyone I was a movie star!"

Did You Know?

Did you know that wheelchair companies used to hire models who didn't have disabilities? Now not many would do that because they realize that they should show real wheelchair users — and pay them for modeling with money or free products.

Ma'rwa Ahteemi: Learning New Ways

Photo by Jacqeline Malonson/AP

Ma'rwa Ahteemi is a long way from home. The 12-year-old from Iraq was injured in the war there when U.S. mortar accidentally hit her home. She has been in the United States getting rehab for several months.

"I feel like a stranger," says Ma'rwa (sounds like "Mattawa"). But Ma'rwa is learning things about independence she wouldn't learn in Iraq, where people with disabilities always stay home. Before her spinal cord injury, Ma'rwa had never even seen another kid in a wheelchair!

Now she knows she can go outside, play with other kids and even help on her family's farm. "I will do the same as before," she says.

Will she be embarrassed? "Why should I be embarrassed?" Ma'rwa asks. "It will be normal for me."

Ma'rwa has done some fun things while in America, including going to two amusement parks. "It's very expensive!" says Ma'rwa, who is used to living in a small village.

When Ma'rwa returns home to Iraq, she will take her Quickie wheelchair and many American supplies that are hard to get there. But her life will be very different from the way it is now. For one thing, Ma'rwa's father doesn't believe girls should learn to read and write. This is an old policy handed down by the former dictator Saddam Hussein, so hopefully the Iraqi people will change their minds about this now that Saddam is out of power. Ma'rwa very much wants to learn Arabic.

Ma'rwa's uncle, Saleh, came with her to America, and he will help teach their family about Ma'rwa's disability. Saleh says Ma'rwa's mom and grandmother will probably want to take care of her more than they need to. They may want to keep her at home. "I can advise them," says Saleh. "It's not nice to stay at home and get lonely. I've seen how it is here, how she can be dependable."

Ma'rwa's house has been rebuilt since she was there, and Ma'rwa is looking forward to seeing it and her family. In addition to her parents, aunts and uncles, she has 16 brothers and sisters. She had 19, but three were killed in the explosion that injured her.

When asked what she would say to a brother or sister if they needed to use a wheelchair, Ma'rwa says she would share with them what she's learned in America. "I would show them, teach them what I can do."

—By Jean Dobbs
Interview by J.R. Carpenter

Mattie Stepanek: Playing After Storms

Mattie Stepanek has always had to fight for his life. Which explains why all this 13-year-old thinks about is peace. "I've always wanted to be a peacemaker," he once said. "Violence is not the answer. Nowadays, we're fighting over little things that in the great scheme of life don't matter."

Mattie was born with a rare type of muscular dystrophy that requires him to use a ventilator. His brothers and sisters all died from this same disease. Although Mattie was the sickest of his brothers and sisters, he has somehow managed to survive. And on more than one occasion, he has grown so desperately sick that doctors didn't think he would pull through.

Which is exactly what was happening to Mattie in the summer of 2000 when he lay in a hospital bed. One day, he was asked if he had one final wish. Wasting no time, Mattie replied that he actually had three wishes: to meet former President Jimmy Carter; to publish the poems he'd been writing since he was 3; and to speak with talk show host Oprah Winfrey about his message of hope and peace.

Within months, all three of Mattie's wishes had become reality. He appeared on "Oprah." He landed a five-book deal with a top publishing house. And, not only did he get a chance to meet Jimmy Carter, he soon became friends with him. Even more importantly, Mattie's condition improved so dramatically that he was able to leave the hospital.

Since then, Mattie has become a popular public speaker and can often be seen on television talk shows, doing book signings and giving motivational speeches for the Muscular Dystrophy Association. His series of five *Heartsongs* books of poetry have sold over 1.5 million copies.

Mattie has always been the type to make something positive out of a negative. "The disease is a curse at first sight, but I wouldn't be me without it," Mattie once said. "I haven't given up. I don't sit in the corner and cry about my life. I make the fullest of it. I go through 'why me' phases. I cry and get upset, but instead of being evil and mad, I say, 'Why not me?' Better me than a kid that has all kinds of stress on his or her life."

When he's not writing poetry or making public appearances, Mattie likes to play video games and collect rocks. He also loves to read and is a huge

Photo courtesy of the Muscular Dystrophy Association

Mattie has written five books of poetry. See page 105 for more about his books.

"Harry Potter" fan. So much so that when he got a chance to meet Emma Watson, who plays Hermione Granger in the Potter movies, he nearly fainted. "I'm still going nuts, saying, 'She touched my hand!'" Mattie said. "When she whipped around, her hair accidentally went into my mouth for a second. I said to my mom, 'I'm never washing this hand or brushing my teeth again.' She said, 'The hand we can work out, but the teeth, sorry. You've got to brush them.'"

Not surprisingly Mattie wants to become a peacemaker just like his friend and role model Jimmy Carter. To the countless people whose lives he has touched, Mattie's words have brought more peace than he realizes. "I want people to know that in every life there are storms," he said. "But we must remember to play after every storm and to celebrate the gift of life as we have it, or else life becomes a task, rather than a gift. We must always listen to the song in our heart and share that song with others."

— *By Ed Oldham*

EDITOR'S NOTE: Just as *Kids on Wheels* was about to be printed, we learned that Mattie lost the struggle for his life. At his funeral, many friends — including former President Jimmy Carter — spoke of Mattie's greatness.

Naomi Catford-Robinson: Joining the Fun

I'm writing about my 10-year-old sister, Naomi, because she can't talk or write by herself. She uses a wheelchair and doesn't use her hands or arms much, and only eats liquids with a g-tube straight into her stomach. But we sure have a full life!

We go camping almost every year, and plug her pump into a thing that uses the van battery to make it work. An orange extension cord runs into our tent, and we hang her bag from the roof. We go hiking — her wheelchair is a super-cool "all-terrain vehicle."

We also go to Mexico, which means taking two weeks of formula, meds and equipment for her Rett Syndrome. Naomi has a special vest with lots of straps that attaches to the seat, because she can't sit without support. She loves swimming in the warm water with her neck float so she can be independent. We even swam with dolphins once. Even though places aren't wheelchair accessible like in this country, there are always lots of people who are willing to carry her and her chair onto the beach, or down the curb.

We go to Lake Tahoe for New Year's. We go cross-country skiing and pull Naomi in a sled, with blankets and pillows. Guess what we secure her with? Bungee cords! Her walker doesn't work in the snow, though.

During the year Naomi plays Challenger Little League baseball with other kids with disabilities. Everyone has a buddy to help them hit the ball and make it around the bases. For a couple of years I was my sister's buddy. She likes baseball, but she loves swimming!

Naomi goes to a swim class for kids with special needs at the YMCA. They have a warm, shallow pool. I used to go with her, but it got boring (I am 12). Naomi and her friends love it. She can move the way she wants to without gravity interfering.

Although she doesn't talk, Naomi communicates with her eyes, facial expressions, sounds, and by waving her arms and legs. She looks at, or touches, YES and NO cards, and can hit buttons, with words and pictures on them, that are connected to taped messages. When we asked her if she wanted other kids who use wheelchairs to know about all the things she does, so they might be able to do them too, she waved wildly with an ear-to-ear grin on her face. That was YES!

— *By Amber Catford-Robinson with Lorna Catford*

Nick Cugini: Future Politician?

At 13, Nick Cugini has learned something that many people don't learn until they're adults — that if you want to change things, then you have to get involved.

Nick is in seventh grade and has already helped make changes at his school. Nick has cerebral palsy, which would make it a challenge to get around the large campus to all his extracurricular activities without a scooter. Luckily, he has one. At home uses a walker.

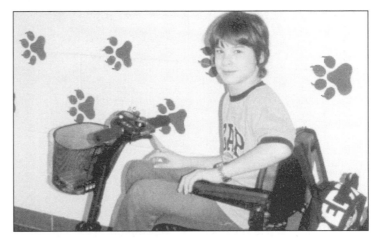

Last year, his first at Truitt Middle School in Houston, Texas, Nick joined the student council. He was also picked to be on the school district superintendent's leadership team. As part of these two groups, Nick suggests ways to make the school better for students. Last year he helped start a cultural fair. This year, the student council wants to make the first day of school nicer for new students.

"We're setting up welcoming committee for new students because when new students come to school, they're not as included as other students," Nick says.

It's a lot of extra work, but it makes Nick feel good to make the school a better place.

Nick's got a lot of friends at school and has been in classes with many of the same kids since first grade. But sometimes new kids notice that he's different when he's zooming around school in a scooter. Nick simply tells them the truth, if they ask why.

"I'll say I have cerebral palsy. I can't walk because my muscles don't work as well," he says.

Nick works very hard to stay healthy. He goes to physical therapy every week. He swims and lifts weights and stretches to keep his muscles strong. When Nick was little, he used a motorized wheelchair. But when he was 5, he was strong enough to walk with a walker. It was a big change for a little boy, and Nick was reluctant.

"I didn't want to," Nick says. "It was really hard. But now it's fine."

When he's not cracking the textbooks or planning a school project, Nick reads — a lot! He's read the entire "Harry Potter" series, and finished the last one in six and one-quarter days. Now he's reading the Redwall books, which are fantasy stories about rats and mice in medieval times. He also likes to play computer games on his Game Cube. One of his favorites is called Civilization 3. Nick likes it especially because it lets him make his own societies.

"You build your civilization, choose the government type and build the cities, the economies, the culture," Nick says. "And you have to deal with other countries."

Someday, Nick might do those things for real. His experience with student council made him want to do even more, maybe even have a career in politics.

"I want to get involved to change the world," Nick says. "I enjoy being part of leadership and being somebody who makes changes."

— By Mariel Garza

Keith and Todd Goldberg: Twin Towers

On the basketball court, Keith and Todd Goldberg, 11, are known as the "twin towers." They earned the nickname not because of their size (actually, they're both fairly small), but due to their big personalities on and off the court. The two brothers have a condition known as spastic diplegia, which causes the muscles in their legs to remain tight. Because they sometimes drag their feet or have trouble raising their knees, walking can be difficult. At school, they usually get around with canes. They first started using wheelchairs when they were 6 years old.

"Now we use our chairs for sports or long trips," says Keith. "It feels good to wheel around and play in a wheelchair. We can both move around pretty quickly."

The twins, who attend fifth grade at

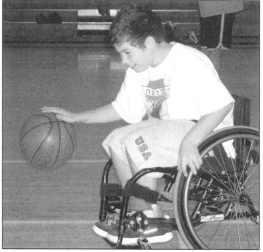

Guess which twin this is! Hint: He wants to build robots.

Evans Elementary in Augusta, Georgia, enjoy competing in wheelchair tennis, basketball and soccer. In order to keep their arms and shoulders strong, they regularly lift weights and do yoga stretches with their father, who also uses a wheelchair due to spastic diplegia. "We've got pretty strong hands and arms," admits Keith.

Todd and Keith are best friends. But they also enjoy competing against one another. "We like racing each other down hills in our chairs," laughs Todd. "We go pretty fast, but it's usually a close tie."

Despite their cheerful demeanor, the Goldberg brothers admit that there are times when they get depressed. "When I think about how I can't do the things that other kids can, I get sad sometimes," says Todd. But, adds Keith, "it makes us happy when we do good things in our chairs, like when we're playing basketball or tennis."

When they're not competing at sports, the twins immerse themselves in their hobbies. Keith enjoys taking photographs and wants to learn how to make videos. Todd likes fixing broken toys and hopes to one day build robots. "When I first got in my chair, I thought about building a robot who would be able to show me all the things I need to learn about my wheelchair and how to make it go," he says.

Getting the knack of using a chair can be difficult at first, adds Todd. "You have to be patient," he says. "It takes awhile to learn everything you need to know."

— *By Ed Oldham*

Cottie Jarrow: Flashing Chrome

Cottie Jarrow loves music — especially the people who make that music. With her mom, Cottie has traveled from her home in Columbus, Ohio, to cities near and far to see her favorite bands. She's got a collection of autographed posters, T-shirts and photos. She even wears a charm bracelet and a pair of gold earrings that were gifts from one of her crushes, Jesse McCartney.

It all started with the Backstreet Boys, which lead to Aaron Carter (brother of Backstreet Boy Nick Carter). Then, Cottie says, "I got hooked on a group called Dream Street." After Dream Street broke up, Cottie and her mom started going to their solo concerts, with a special interest in Jesse, Greg Raposo and, now, Stevie Brock.

Since Cottie uses a wheelchair — and since almost everyone else at these concerts is standing up — Cottie has to sit in front in order to see. *Right* up front — at her first Dream Street concert, Cottie's toes were touching the stage. When Greg, one of the singers, sang a ballad, he slid off the stage, held Cottie's face in his hands and sang directly to her.

As the only wheelchair-using fan sitting near the stage for so many shows, Cottie is very recognizable. Cottie's mom calls it "flashing chrome." That's an expression borrowed from motorcycle riders — she means they use Cottie's chair to attract attention. "The way I see it, it works against her often enough, it might as well work in her favor when it can," says her mom.

Cottie has a cockatiel who sometimes sits on her shoulder. "He has feathers that stick straight up — so I named him Chris, because one of the singers I like, Chris Trousdale, has spikey hair."

Is music the most important thing to Cottie right now? You decide. "I saw a

Cottie poses with Dillon Kondor, guitarist for Jesse McCartney.

Britney Spears concert a couple of years ago," she says. "That was before I discovered boys."

But life isn't all boy bands. Cottie and her mom have traveled all over the country together. Cottie especially likes aquariums and oceanariums, and hopes to become a marine biologist. "I think marine life is really interesting and beautiful," she says. "On vacation to Hawaii, we got to see whales and spinner dolphins up close. I had my picture taken with a huge dolphin at Sea Life Park. And we went to Hanauma Bay, where I tried snorkeling for the first time."

Cottie is 13 and has cerebral palsy. She uses a power chair, and communicates through a combination of speech and her own sign language. The Internet helps a lot, too. With e-mail and instant messaging, Cottie can chat with her friends directly, without an adult interpreting.

Another way Cottie can express her feelings is through poetry. At right is a poem she wrote when she was 10.

— *By Laura Kaminker*

Everyone Is Different
by Cottie Jarrow

Everyone is different,
Everyone I know.
Everyone is different.
I think that is so.
Everyone is different,
Just like you and me.
So I'm just like everyone
Because no one's just like me!

Lauren Gunder: Tomboy Spirit

Forget dresses and Barbies and pretty pink things. Lauren Gunder would rather have blue jeans, Matchbox cars and baseball — especially baseball.

Lauren is 13 and lives in a town near Atlanta, Georgia. She has osteopetrosis, which means her bones are weak and break easily. She has broken more than 20 since she was a baby. Lauren must be extra careful not to put too much pressure on her bones, so she uses a wheelchair. She is also legally blind and hearing impaired.

All of these things might discourage a lot of people from playing sports. Not Lauren. She has been playing with her team, the Braves, since she was 9 years old. The team is part of the Miracle League Association, which builds special rubber fields for disabled girls and boys

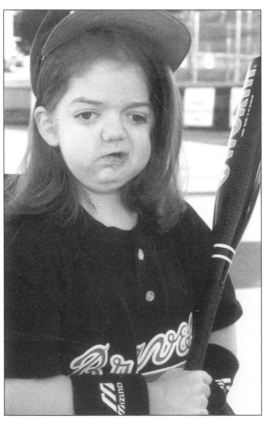

to play baseball. She loves the freedom where she doesn't have to worry about getting hurt.

"It's kinda cool I get to play since I'm in a wheelchair," Lauren says. And it's just a whole lot of fun, too. "It's cool to be with your friends and to get to throw things."

Lauren is in eighth grade at Trickum Middle School. The school has a program for visually impaired kids mixed in with the rest of the school. She has friends in the program and out of the program and in different grades. She spends at least an hour each night talking with her friends, sometimes having a three-way call.

Lauren's friends are among the most important things in her life, and have helped her through a lot of hard times. Last year Lauren could get around with a walker and could bat for the Braves standing up. But her last break, at the start of seventh grade, was so bad it put her in a body cast for most of the school year. After that, she had to use a wheelchair full time. The change was difficult for Lauren.

"I didn't want to do it at all," Lauren says. Her best friend, Patricia, helped cheer her up. "Patricia had some problems also, so we would compare notes and make jokes."

Lauren likes jokes and especially loves pulling practical jokes. Her favorite one was when she ran into her friend's father in the grocery store one day. He said he was buying chicken and corn for dinner that night. When Lauren got home, she called her friend and told her she was psychic. To prove it she told the friend exactly what her father was going to make for dinner. Later that night, her friend called back amazed!

Lauren's philosophy is to use humor to get through the difficult parts of life. "When someone's having a hard time, my job is to make a joke," Lauren says. It works when she's feeling bad also. "It makes me feel better when I laugh. I can make fun of myself."

— *By Mariel Garza*

Tyler Gaul: Free to Roam

Tyler Gaul would never think of letting his muscular dystrophy prevent him from helping out on his parent's 180-acre farm. But three years ago, when Tyler began relying on a wheelchair, that's exactly what started to happen. He'd just sit around his house and grow frustrated watching his three younger brothers and parents doing their chores. Tyler longed to lend a hand. One morning, just after the fall harvest two years ago, Tyler told his mother that more than anything else, he wished he had a tractor to help him get around the farm.

When his mother happened to mention Tyler's wish to a friend, it wasn't long before neighbors and family members in New Vienna, Iowa, began scouring the countryside, collecting junked and discarded farm machinery. They decided to build Tyler a special tractor that he could operate while sitting in his wheelchair. "Everyone got involved," recalls Tyler.

Many months later, Tyler, now 13, was the owner of a custom-made, one-of-a-kind John Deere tractor, complete with a hydraulic ramp that can be raised and lowered, enabling him to drive his power wheelchair up into the cab. Instead of a steering wheel, he uses a joystick. To move forward, he pushes it forward. When he pulls the joystick back, the tractor goes backward. If he lets go of it, the machine immediately stops. "It's kinda like a dream come true," says Tyler. "I use it to carry food out to the field hands and haul hay in from the field."

Tyler's tractor, nicknamed "the magnificent green freedom machine," has helped make adjusting to the wheelchair a bit easier. In November 2003, Tyler underwent a lengthy five-hour surgery during which two metal rods were placed along his spine to help give him

Photos courtesy of Pride Mobility

better posture. (Sitting up straight can be difficult for those with muscular dystrophy, who often get pneumonia because they can't take deep breaths.) "Sometimes things can be tough," explains Tyler. "But you have to keep pushing yourself. You can't ever stop."

From the sounds of it, Tyler, an avid sports fan who manages a local Little League team, isn't about to stop pushing — not himself or others. "He does whatever he can around the farm," says his mom. "He's really a driving force here. He's constantly motivating everybody, especially his brothers, to always do their best."

—By Ed Oldham

Emily Shanahan: Independent Queen

Emily Shanahan is living proof that you can navigate high school using a wheelchair and find independence and friends apart from family — just like any other teenager. A 15-year-old who lives in West Carrollton, Ohio, Emily started high school in 2003 and immediately joined several groups, including Writer's Ink, a writer's club. The club is currently penning a play about a fairy tale with a twist, and her costume will incorporate her wheelchair.

"I do the unexpected thing: I smile and say 'hi.'"

Acting and modeling come naturally to Emily, who has done both since she was a young girl, even appearing in a gospel musical movie.

Diagnosed at 18 months with cerebral palsy, Emily got her first wheelchair at 5. She uses a power wheelchair and DragonDictate, voice-activated computer software. Emily's many years in public school taught her the best way to approach nondisabled peers.

"People are curious about me," she says. "They're not sure how to react. They're not sure if I've got brain damage or only physical problems. A couple of times I've come into a classroom and everyone's turned and looked at me, even the teacher. Then I do the unexpected thing: I smile and say 'hi,'" she says with a laugh. Emily usually has to go up to people and start conversations, but once they get past their initial discomfort, they realize she is no different from them, except she uses a chair. Her outgoing personality has proven to be a benefit in high school.

"I have a license to be weird anyway, so I take advantage of that," says Emily, referring to her passion for ancient history, especially Egypt and its "famous, independent queens." "So many people came up against so many insurmountable odds and they persevered anyway," she explains.

Outside of school, Emily is a big fan of therapeutic horseback riding and likes spending time with friends from the Fellowship of Christian Students. Last summer at camp, she braved an 800-foot zip line across a lake several times.

Last fall, her parents equipped her wheelchair with a speaker cell phone and she got to go shopping for a couple of hours with a girlfriend and no parents in sight. A teenager's dream come true!

Emily plans to attend college and earn a degree in family counseling and Biblical history, with hopes of becoming a family therapist. And she already has some advice: "There will be rough spots, but in a bad situation, a good thing can come out of it — you've just got to look for it."
— *By Kathe A. Conti*

role model

Marc Obletz: From the Heart

The way Marc Obletz sees it, attitude is everything. Which explains why this 19-year-old high school senior has spent much of his life not only cultivating an upbeat outlook on life, but also trying to spread good vibes wherever he goes. "I've always been enthusiastic and happy about life," says Marc. "Nothing stops me."

Marc has cerebral palsy and has used a wheelchair ever since a surgery on his spine to relieve the tightness in his arms made walking too painful. "I later found out that only one in 10 people actually survive that surgery, so I consider myself one of the lucky ones," says Marc, whose speech is slightly slurred as a result of his CP.

Marc and his twin brother, who also has cerebral palsy, were adopted shortly after birth and were raised in a very encouraging home. Marc credits his adoptive parents with helping him believe there's nothing he can't do. "I've had really supportive parents who have raised me to live an independent life," he says. "With that kind of support, you can easily succeed. That was especially helpful when I was younger and I felt I was the only one with a disability."

These days, Marc has become something of a living legend at Half Hollow Hills High School in Dix Hills, New York. He's a member of the National Honor Society, serves on several disability advisory councils, has won college scholarship money, and was chosen to appear in a public service announcement on TV with actor William H. Macy. But his favorite activity over the past few years has involved working as an assistant coach for his school's varsity basketball team.

"Before each game I give the players

a motivational pep talk," says Marc, who is looking forward to attending college and one day working in the field of video production. "I'm a good speaker. But I think the reason I get such a good response from the players is because when I speak to them, it really comes from my heart, and they know it." It probably shouldn't come as a big surprise that Marc's pep talks have helped the team win so many games. One of his favorite hobbies involves reading motivational stories about people who have overcome enormous obstacles in their lives, and he often uses these stories in his speeches.

Asked if he has any motivational words for kids who may be experiencing the kinds of situations he faced when he was younger, Marc just closes his eyes and smiles. A moment later, he announces, "One of the most important things is to never be negative, because it's not going to get you anywhere. Try to always be outgoing. And speak up for yourself. If you need something, don't ever be afraid to ask for it."

Marc (left) says his supportive family helps him succeed.

— By Ed Oldham

LeAnn Shannon:
From Athlete to Author

Imagine you're a star athlete. You've broken records in every sport you've played. You were the youngest U.S. Olympic track athlete ever, and the youngest gold-medal winner of any country. What do you do next?

If you're LeAnn Shannon, you retire from racing at age 18 and start writing books.

LeAnn, who had a spinal cord injury as an infant, started wheelchair racing when she was only 12 years old. She trained four to six hours a day, six days a week. Like any athlete, LeAnn was driven to compete, but winning races wasn't her only motivation. She says, "One of the reasons I went to the Olympics was to show people that just because you're young, and just because you have a disability, doesn't mean you can't do anything as well as an adult or someone who isn't disabled."

when she was 4 years old. She quickly became one of the top junior athletes in the country. After seeing the wheelchair races in the 1992 Olympics on TV, LeAnn decided to train for the 1996 Olympics and Paralympics in Atlanta.

To qualify for the national team, LeAnn competed against adult racers

The intense preparation paid off: In Atlanta, LeAnn set two world records and won four medals — three gold and one silver. Everyone expected LeAnn to come up big in the next Paralympics, in 2000. Instead, she retired. "Training overlapped with registering for college," she says. "I figured college was more important."

role model

"Just because you're young, and just because you have a disability, doesn't mean you can't do anything as well as an adult or someone who isn't disabled."

Now, at the University of Central Florida in Orlando, LeAnn has a double major in computer sciences and English. That combination covers both of LeAnn's passions — writing and video gaming.

LeAnn writes fantasy novels, along the lines of "The Lord of the Rings" series, written by J.R.R. Tolkien. She finished her first book for her senior project in high school.

The computer science classes feed what LeAnn calls her "gaming habit." She loves MMORPGs, or mass multiplayer online role-playing games, like Dark Ages Camelot. "Sometimes you can't write anything, no matter how hard you try," she says. "I play games to clear my mind. Whenever I'm not doing schoolwork or writing, I'm gaming."

Because it's very difficult to earn a living as a writer, most writers also need another job. LeAnn thinks that developing MMORPGs and writing fantasy novels would be the perfect dual career.

LeAnn plays a friendly game of basketball now and again, but she doesn't miss competing. Going professional, she feels, "is a sure-fire way to knock every last bit of fun out of a sport."

A positive part of racing was traveling all over the world. "It definitely gave me a love for travel," LeAnn says. "I can't stand staying in the same place for more than a few weeks. I have to go somewhere, even if it's just two hours away to visit my family."

One of LeAnn's favorite places is England. " I had always wanted to visit the country where Tolkien lived," she says. "I originally wanted to go to Oxford University, but was slapped with the reality that there were far too many stairs." Last summer LeAnn went to Europe on her own for three weeks, visiting Vienna, Prague, London, Dublin, and Paris.

But LeAnn's favorite places — in this or any other world — exist only in her imagination.

— *By Laura Kaminker*

Kyle Glozier: Changing the World

When Kyle Glozier was 8 years old, he visited the national headquarters of ADAPT in Denver, Colorado. ADAPT is an organization of people with disabilities who fight for equal rights for all disabled people. Kyle knew right away he had found his place. "I felt like I belonged," he says.

Since then, Kyle has marched in demonstrations, given speeches all over

Kyle talks with Justin Dart, a great disability rights leader.

the country, testified before Congress, debated with a movie star, and appeared on national television.

Kyle is now 18 years old and a senior in high school. He plans to study law so he can advocate for children with disabilities. "There's no distinction between my regular life and my life as an activist," he says. "I'm in this 24/7."

The members of ADAPT want Congress to pass a law called the Medicaid Community Attendant Services and Supports Act, known as MiCASSA. Right now, Medicaid (the public health system) does not pay for long-term personal attendants. Because of this, people with disabilities who *could* live in their own homes, go to school and work, *if* they had a personal attendant — but who cannot afford one — often are forced to

live in nursing homes. (This includes children and teenagers.) Kyle says MiCASSA would "free our people from being locked up in the name of care."

Kyle has cerebral palsy and requires an attendant, so this is a personal issue for him. But Kyle knows that he is part of something much larger — the disability rights movement.

Four years ago, Kyle testified before a Congressional committee, against a law that would have weakened accessibility requirements. Testifying on the other side was the movie actor and director Clint Eastwood. He also used to be the mayor of Carmel, California.

Kyle used his Liberator communication device, which converts typed words into spoken speech, to answer questions from members of Congress. His intelligence and energy opened a lot of people's eyes. But Mr. Eastwood wasn't too happy about being upstaged by a 14-year-old.

During a break, Eastwood approached Kyle and said, "I have a son named Kyle." Kyle looked him straight in the eye and replied, "So?"

Then Eastwood reached for Kyle's communication device, asking, "How do you make this thing work?" Kyle promptly smacked his hand!

Speaking through the Liberator, Kyle said, "This is not a toy. It's my touch-talker."

Finally, Eastwood took Kyle seriously, and they debated some of the issues.

After his impressive performance in Washington, Kyle was chosen to address the 2000 Democratic National Convention about MiCASSA. The convention was held at the Staples Center in Los Angeles — where the Lakers play. "First the moderator told me there were 35,000 people there," says Kyle. "Then he made me even more nervous by saying that another 1.5 million people would be watching

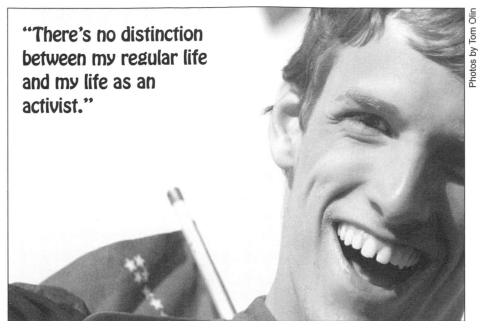

"There's no distinction between my regular life and my life as an activist."

Photos by Tom Olin

So far, Kyle's most famous speech has been to 35,000 people at the 2000 Democratic National Convention. In the photo below, his shirt says it all: "Disabled and Proud."

on television." But Kyle conquered the butterflies in his stomach and gave a stirring speech. The crowd jumped to its feet with thunderous applause.

For young people who are drawn to activism, Kyle has this advice: "First, be informed — watch the news and read the newspaper. Get involved with your local Center for Independent Living. If they don't do a lot of advocacy, get involved with ADAPT. Most states have local chapters — you can find your state's contact person at www.adapt.org."

Kyle is also a writer. He's working on a novel featuring junior detective Ben Zoom. Ben has cerebral palsy, and his sidekick Mike uses a wheelchair. Ben Zoom is Kyle's "alter ego" — he has adventures that his creator hasn't gotten around to yet.

— *By Laura Kaminker*

• To see and hear Kyle testifying before the Congressional committee, go to: www.tripil.com/tripil/kyle-adantce.html

• To see and hear Kyle speaking at the 2000 Democratic National Convention, go to: www.tripil.com/tripil/kyle-demo.html

Why Play Sports?

The first reason to play wheelchair sports can be summed up in one simple word — FUN. Come to think of it, FUN is the second, third and fourth reasons, too.

What Else?

Now you're thinking, OK, so there's fun, fun, fun and fun. And why do I want to do this?

If you're like a lot of people with disabilities (not just kids), you're the only person you know who uses a wheelchair. Maybe there's one other kid in your school, maybe two. But chances are they're not even your friends.

When you play wheelchair sports, you meet lots of other kids who all have something in common — you all use wheelchairs. It's good that everyone goes to school together — kids who wheel, kids who walk, kids who use crutches — that's the way it should be. But it feels good to be in a place where everyone is more like you. To be part of a community. Wheelchair sports can give you a feeling of belonging.

Still Not Convinced?

You're a tough sell. Luckily, there are a few more reasons.

While you're having fun and meeting other kids who use chairs, you'll get all

It's all about the fun!

the other benefits of sports, too. You'll get stronger. You'll gain confidence in yourself and your abilities. You'll learn skills that will help you in everything you do, like teamwork and setting (and achieving) goals. You'll get healthier. You'll enjoy your life more.

Who knows, you may turn out to be a great athlete. You can work hard, train with a coach, and go to the Junior Nationals — the national competition for people with disabilities under 18 years old. From there, there are national competitions and tournaments for each sport, and international multi-sport competitions like the World Wheelchair Games.

The ultimate competition is the

You'll get healthier. You'll enjoy your life more. And who knows, you may turn out to be a great athlete.

Teammates Jill Moore and Sean Burns hustle for the ball.

Paralympics. The Paralympics is the world's largest sporting event. It's held after the Olympics, in the same city and in the same facilities as the Olympics. Paralympic athletes are the absolute best at what they do.

But you don't have be a future Paralympian to play sports. You don't even have to decide if that's something you'll ever want to try for. In fact, you only have to remember one word.

Hint: It's the first, second, third and fourth reasons to try wheelchair sports.

Where Do I Begin?

There are adaptive sports programs all over the country. Different programs offer different sports — what's available will depend on where you live. You never know what you'll find unless you look.

At the end of this chapter, we've made a list of the best-known programs. Check it out — see if one is near you and give them a call. But new programs are spring-

ing up all the time. If you don't find what you want on our list, make your own!

Start with www...

• Start with the Internet. If you don't have access at home, it's worth a trip to your local library. Try searching for "adaptive sports" or "wheelchair sports." You can narrow your search with the name of a big city near where you live, or the name of a sport that you'd like to try. For example, you can try "wheelchair sports Chicago" or "wheelchair basketball."

• Some of the best adaptive sports programs in the country are run by rehab hospitals. Even though you're not sick, look in the phone book under "hospitals, rehabilitation" or "physical therapy." You can try the Internet for this, too. When you find something in your area, you or your parents can call. Ask for the sports and recreation department — and ask them what's available for juniors.

• Try the parks and recreation department in your town or city. Some have terrific adaptive sports programs. It might be called "therapeutic recreation," or ask if they run a sports program for kids with physical disabilities.

• Call your local YMCA. If they don't have an adaptive sports program, they might know who does.

• Some states include adaptive sports program as part of their regular public school programs. This means kids who use wheelchairs play on teams just like nondisabled kids. They practice after school, go to other schools for games, have tournaments — the works. Unfortunately, not enough states do this, but the number is growing.

In some schools — for example, in Minnesota — the adaptive sports programs are for high school students. This could give you a goal to work for — learn how to play wheelchair basketball

Michael Timpa focuses on the finish line.

now, so you can make the team when you're older. Other states, like Louisiana, start at kindergarten and go right up to high school graduation. Right now, Minnesota, Georgia and Louisiana have adaptive sports programs.

Ask An Expert

Joel Berman, who runs Adaptive Adventures, says: "I like to start with the activity. I don't say, I'm in a wheelchair, what can I do. I say, I have an 8-year-old, what do 8-year-olds like to do? There are some things you might cross off the list, but you're still left with many options. Yes, it would be easier if you didn't have any special needs. But don't think it can't happen if you do."

Joel recommends speaking to people who know about a sport, especially when it comes to outdoor activities. He explains, "It's a lot easier to teach someone who knows all about a sport a little about disability, than to teach someone about a sport." For example, a disabled skiing instructor is a ski expert who *also* knows how to adapt skiing for different disabilities. "If you go to a kayak shop," says Joel, "you'll talk to someone who knows all about kayaking and canoeing. They'll think, OK, what does this person need to make this work? The same is true for sailing, horseback riding, skiing, and many outdoor sports."

If at first you don't succeed: PERSIST!! You might not strike gold on your first Web search or phone call. Finding a program that's right for you might require a little determination and your best detective skills. But most kids who play wheelchair sports will tell you: It's totally worth the effort.

Jessica Lucas

Jessica, with her proud dad, holds her "Rookie of the Year" Award .

profile

Anyone who needs convincing of the power of wheelchair sports should meet Jessica Lucas.

Jessica is 9 years old, and lives in Brentwood, California. When Jessica was an infant, she had cancer on her spinal cord that paralyzed her.

The cancer, and the treatments to cure it, left Jessica very weak. When she was 1 year old, she could barely hold her head up for five minutes.

When Jessica was 5, she started playing basketball. Her parents and her occupational therapist noticed the difference right away. Her strength, balance and endurance shot up. She had so much more energy. Before long, the time Jessica spent in therapy was cut in half.

Out of Her Shell

There have been other benefits, too. Jessica has always been very shy. All her life, she had endured a lot of medical procedures, and she was very afraid of strangers. Once when someone had to adjust her wheelchair while she was in it, Jessica was so frightened that all she could do was curl up and cry.

Now when Jessica goes to the doctor, she's not afraid. She talks to the people around her and asks questions. Jessica's teachers and her school aides have all noticed the difference. Jessica had been like a turtle, hiding in her shell. Now she's a butterfly, flitting around and enjoying the world.

Jessica is the youngest player on her basketball team at BORP, which stands for Bay Area Outreach and Recreation Program. She started on the 5-foot team (that's the height of the basket), then graduated to 8-foot. She plays in her everyday wheelchair. She is also beginning track, using one of BORP's racing chairs.

Jessica also has a handcycle, which BORP helped her family get. She rides in a park near her home, or with her friends at BORP.

Jessica's Pal Chester

Jessica is the only student at Discovery Bay Elementary school who uses a wheelchair. Sometimes that makes her feel a little lonely. When that happens, she talks about her feelings with her mom. Jessica says, "When I first started kindergarten, I was kind of scared. But now I have a lot of friends."

One of her best friends is Chester, her Border terrier. Jessica used to visit Chester and some other puppies where they lived. When the owners learned that Chester had a disability, they gave him to Jessica as a gift. Jessica says, "I can't walk, and he has a hole in his heart, so we are almost alike. We were meant to be together."

Jessica thinks kids who use wheelchairs should try sports "because it's really fun. If you don't know anyone else in wheelchairs, you'll meet more people. And because they're in wheelchairs too, you can talk about it."

Archery

Almost anyone can shoot a bow and arrow. Wheelchair archers who have full upper-body strength use the exact same equipment as standing archers — they just shoot sitting down.

Quadriplegics, people with cerebral palsy and amputees can all shoot, too. There are "compound bows," which require less strength, and adaptive equipment to help you hold them. There's even a device that lets archers shoot with their teeth. Many highly competitive archers are mouth shooters.

Wheelchair archers brag about their sport because it's fully integrated — disabled and nondisabled archers compete side by side at national archery events, under the exact same rules. All certified archery instructors in the United States are trained in disabled shooting, and lots of adapted sports programs offer archery, too.

Layton LaFevers

Layton LaFevers will try, play and do nearly anything. He loves fishing, shooting his bow and arrow, swimming, camping, riding his handcycle, and — as his mom says — "anything and everything that has to do with people and being outside." Layton, who is 7 years old and has spina bifida, says, "I go exploring. I go everywhere. I'm never afraid!"

Layton's favorite sport is wheelchair basketball. When he started, he was so small that he couldn't shoot. At his first tournament, Layton's dad explained defense by drawing a diagram on the back of a place mat at a restaurant. The next day on the court, Layton put up strong "D."

Layton said, "I did good, but there were big kids, with big chairs. We would try to stop them from getting the ball. We skidded our chairs up there, and tried to stop them, but I couldn't stop one of them, because he was so fast. But I tried! Next time I'll do it."

Layton's team, the Junior Rollin' Razorbacks, placed fourth in the nation in their division. Layton's hustle and his love of the game earned him the Spirit Award for the National Tournament. His dad said that Layton "had more fun than I ever could have imagined."

Some people thought Layton's parents were crazy for letting such a tiny guy play ball with kids who were so much bigger than him. But you might as well try and stop a tornado. His dad says, "People give us, his parents, so much credit for it. But when you meet Layton, you see it isn't us. If anything, we're the anchor that he's dragging behind him."

profile

Basketball

Basketball takes top prize for most popular wheelchair sport. You'll find a basketball team at almost every adaptive sports program. Everyone should try playing wheelchair basketball at least once — whether or not they use a wheelchair.

Basketball is also the oldest organized wheelchair sport. In the United States, the National Wheelchair Basketball Association (NWBA) has been around for almost 60 years. There are wheelchair basketball teams all over the country and all over the world.

There are dozens of junior teams —

Photo courtesy of Fanlight Productions

kids start in kindergarten and play all the way up to high school graduation. There's also a league for college students.

For younger kids, the baskets may be

View from Center Court *By Cully Mason*

A sudden rush passes through your whole body as the coach signals you into the game. The pressure is on.

Everyone counts on you to play to your maximum potential, but you know you're ready from all the intense practices over the past months. You pass the boundary from spectator to participant, and all stress and worry leaves you. You are thankful for that because in this fast game of wheelchair basketball, stress can only slow you down.

The ball is in-bounded and the shot clock awakes. The game is alive and breathing, and it pulses with every steady beat of the ball. You know your mission, and you proceed with every push of the wheel.

The ball shoots across half-court into the protective hands of the point guard. It is time to fulfill your mission as you set up for the perfect screen shot. You see the game clearly — like a pirate with a treasure map — as the point guard gives the play signal.

You move swiftly yet mindfully

"The game is alive and breathing, and it pulses with every steady beat of the ball."

and call for the ball. As soon as you feel the rubber grip on your fingertips, all of the pressure and worry shoots back through your body. All eyes are on you as you recognize your duty to the team. Sweat builds on your face and eyes. Your arms start to tense and then lift off in the direction of the goal. In an instant the ball is released from your hand and you go from the crucial figure of the game to completely helpless, for the ball is no longer in your control. You watch in suspense as the ball volleys on the sides of the rim once ... twice — and then it falls, making a much-anticipated sound through the net.

The pressure subsides as the scoreboard boasts your success. Mission accomplished. Could it be just a dream? No, just one of thousands of moments spent on the Blaze Sports Junior Wheelchair Basketball team.

Blaze Sports, a nonprofit organization destined to improve the wheelchair world through sports, can be contacted through its Web site at www.blazesports.com.

Cully Mason, who is 16 and has spina bifida, lives in Monroe, Georgia. He attends George Walton Academy and also participates in track.

5 feet or 8 feet high. Most people start playing with the regulation basket (10 feet high) when they're 13 or 14 years old. You can get started in your everyday chair, and many junior teams have sports chairs that players can use.

Chairs designed for basketball are a little taller than every day chairs (you can guess why), and the wheels are "cambered." Cambered means instead of being straight up and down, the wheels are at an angle.

Of course the game is adapted for wheelchair play. For example, players have to stay firmly seated at all times. Some kids might be able to lift themselves off their seat a little, but to keep things fair, that's not allowed. Other than those kinds of details, wheelchair basketball is the same sport as stand-up basketball. Except some people think it's more fun.

Wheelchair basketball can get super competitive. There are national and international tournaments, and, of course, the Paralympics. But hundreds of kids all over the country play for fun and exercise. If you're like a lot of kids, once you try it, you'll keep coming back.

If you get discouraged, listen to Elizabeth Hassler's story. She first tried wheelchair basketball when she was 8 years old. Elizabeth, who has cerebral palsy, found it too difficult to be fun. After a few tries, she was disappointed and stopped going to BORP.

BORP stands for Bay Area Outreach and Recreational Program — in this case, accent on the *outreach*. Someone from BORP called Elizabeth's home, asking when she was going to come back. And they kept calling. Elizabeth's mother finally said, "You'd better go, or they'll never leave us alone!"

Now she loves it and plays every Saturday, traveling by herself on the BORP van from her home in Oakland, California.

Kiss My Wheels

Kiss My Wheels is a terrific introduction to competitive basketball — and to the healing power of friends on wheels.

The one-hour film follows a season of the Zia Hot Shots from early practice to the national finals, so there's plenty of great hoops to watch. But it's also about kids with disabilities finding a place they feel accepted and cool.

They talk honestly about loss and pain they've experienced (school was

Photo courtesy of Fanlight Productions

"vicious and cruel and mean") but they're a spunky team that pulls together when times get tough ("it's family!").

The coach, Judge Pat Murdoch, is a wheeler, and a great role model on and off the court. And he's got a knack for keeping shame out of the game. "Whether it's a flat tire or a leaking catheter, we can deal with it," he says. "It is not embarrassing, it is part of life."

Due to some mature themes, this film may not be appropriate for very young children. The video is available for purchase ($249) or rental ($60) from Fanlight Productions in Boston; 800-937-4113 or www.fanlight.com. The filmmakers can be reached through Thunder Road Productions at www.thunder prod.com.

Boccia

The object of boccia — pronounced either "bah-chee" or "bah-cha" — is to place a small leather ball as close as possible to white target ball. The white ball is known as a "jack." Some players throw the leather ball, others shoot it down a ramp. Either way, the idea is to get more balls closer to the jack than your opponent does.

This game is all about precision, accuracy and eye-hand coordination. So it may surprise you to learn that most people who play boccia have cerebral palsy (CP). The challenge lies not in speed or strength, but in concentration and muscle control.

CP athletes all over the world take great pride in their game, which is an official Paralympic sport.

Fencing

Fencing is kind of an oddball. Most wheelchair sports are fast-motion and high-speed, but fencers' wheels stay perfectly still. In fact, the chairs are locked into metal frames to make sure they don't move.

All the chair-handling skills you learn in basketball, racing or tennis won't help you in this sport. Fencing is all about what you have upstairs — it requires a high degree of concentration and mental focus. Some wheelchair fencers compare it to chess, a "mental sport."

Most adapted sports programs don't offer fencing, because the equipment is expensive and the sport isn't easy to learn. If you want to try wheelchair fencing, contact the Shepherd Center in Atlanta. Also if you let your local adapted sports center know you're interested, they might have some ideas. You can see some photos of wheelchair fencing, and get more info at http://mywebpage. netscape.com/wcfencer/.

Field

Michael Timpa, in a secure field chair, throws the discus.

The main field events are shot put, discus, softball throw and javelin. Field events are a fun way to build strength, concentration and coordination. Each event has its own technique, but the idea is always the same: Throw the object as far as you can.

Players compete according to their age, size and functional ability, so someone with full use of his or her upper body wouldn't compete against a quadriplegic. Field events are usually done at the track, so while you're trying out a racing chair, ask about the shot put, too.

Football

All you need to play wheelchair football is a bunch of people in chairs, a football, a gym, and someone who knows the rules. (You can also play outside on a hardtop, but then padding and skin protection becomes more important in case of spills.) It's not as organized as wheelchair basketball or racing — there aren't many official teams or scheduled tournaments — but that doesn't stop people from playing it.

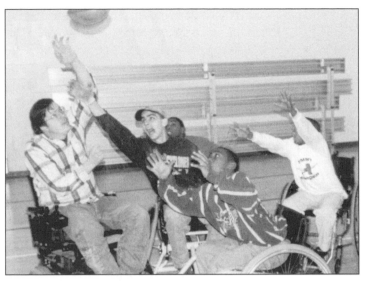

Wheelchair football is mainly a passing game. Field goals and punts are passed instead of kicked, and a "tackle" is touching two hands on the ball-carrier's upper body. If you have enough players, the official game is six on a side, but you can play with any amount — just split up into offense and defense, and you're good to go.

Matt McLaughlin has tried tons of wheelchair sports and activities, and wheelchair football is his hands-down favorite. (See Matt's profile on page 38.) If you have a chance, try the game — see if you agree.

To order more copies of Kids on Wheels, have parents, teachers or therapists call **888-850-0344, ext. 209**

Handcycling

Handcycling might be the world's most accessible sport.

While many wheelchair sports are strictly competitive, handcycling is mostly recreational. It's great exercise, lots of fun, and not difficult to learn. If you have a handcycle, you can bike with your family or your friends, whether or not they have disabilities.

Bikes are lightweight and travel easily, so if your family takes bikes on vacations, yours can come, too. And many bikes are adjustable, so they grow along with you.

One major drawback is that handcycles are very expensive. There are foundations that donate handcycles to disabled kids, and many adaptive sports organizations loan or rent bikes. You also might find a good used bike that someone else has outgrown. One mom had a creative idea about how to get her daughter a handcycle (see next page).

If you love cycling so much that cruising around your local park just isn't enough — or if you're the type who just *has* to compete in *everything* — there is some competitive handcycling, too. In 2004, the National Junior Wheelchair Games will include handcycling for the first time.

But whether or not you ever want to race, try handcycling. It's such a popular sport — and once you feel the wind in your face, you'll know why.

Ryan Wright

profile

When Ryan Wright got on a handcycle at a Colorado Junior Wheelchair Sports Camp, the counselors practically had to pry him off. A few weeks later, Ryan called his friends at Adaptive Adventures to ask if he could borrow the bike for his family's vacation. Ryan, who is 9, rode all around the campgrounds with his two older brothers. Ryan says, "It was awesome."

Like a lot of kids with spina bifida, Ryan doesn't use a wheelchair all the time. But he's a high-energy, athletic guy, so wheels are essential equipment. Ryan has played wheelchair tennis, basketball and rugby. At camp, Ryan won a trophy for being the most aggressive rugby player. And if you've ever seen rugby, that's really saying something!

Ryan plays in an everyday chair that he outgrew. His parents had it rigged up for sports play, so now they don't have to get Ryan's chair repaired after every game.

Ryan lives in Colorado, and he's been skiing since he was 3 years old. He's one of the youngest kids to use a monoski. Ryan skis like he does everything: fast and wild.

Ryan doesn't watch a lot of TV — he'd rather be outside — but if the TV is on, it's turned to ESPN. He loves baseball, dividing his loyalties between the Rockies and the Yankees. And if there are no games, Ryan can always play with his dog, a chocolate Lab named Chance.

Ryan is in fourth grade at West Jefferson Elementary School. He likes school, especially math — even though it's an indoor "sport."

Photo courtesy of Adaptive Adventures

Thank You

I Love My New Bike!
Love, Rachel

The Perfect Gift

Rachel Rassmussen's mom found the perfect bike for Rachel on a handcycling Web site called www.bike-on.com (don't forget the dash). She really wanted to get Rachel the bike, but it was too expensive. So she came up with a plan.

Christine Rasmussen, Rachel's mom, gave Rachel a birthday party. On the invitations, Christine wrote that she was trying to purchase a bicycle for Rachel. She asked people, instead of bringing a gift, to contribute something toward that goal. The birthday donations raised more than half the price of the handcycle.

Later, Christine took a picture of Rachel on her new bike. She put the photo on cards that said, "Thank you, I love my new bike!" and sent one to everyone who donated. Now Christine puts Rachel's little sister, Reanna, in a bike trailer and they all go for a ride together.

Horseback Riding

There's nothing like being around horses. Horses are sensitive, intelligent animals. Playing wheelchair sports is great, but interacting with a living, feeling creature can be a very special experience.

Besides being fun, horseback riding is also very good for you. It improves balance and posture, and helps the rider become more mobile and independent.

There are adaptive riding programs (sometimes called therapeutic riding) all over the country. Instructors use special saddles, ramps and other adaptations to work with people who have all kinds of disabilities. Many programs also teach you how to groom and care for horses.

There are also competitive horse riding events, called equestrian competitions. Riders compete against people with similar disabilities. In the Paralympics, there are two equestrian competitions: the set test and the freestyle test. In the set test, the rider moves the horse through a series of markers, performing specific movements. The freestyle test is performed with music, and judged on both technical skills and artistic impression.

If you like animals and being outdoors, see Chapter 4 for more info.

Outdoor Adventures

Try to think of an outdoor adventure activity that a person who uses a wheelchair *hasn't* done. You'll be thinking for a long, long time — and you'll probably never come up with one.

Scuba diving, rock climbing, mountain biking, sailing, whitewater rafting, water-skiing, fishing, camping, hunting, dog-sledding, kayaking — you name it, people with disabilities do it. There are disabled mountain climbers, championship sailors, even rodeo riders.

The best way to try any of these activities is through an adaptive recreation program. They have the equipment, the know-how and the experience to get you going. Most programs sponsor camps or trips where you can try everything. Some programs are more specialized — like those that teach sailing or fishing. And some are just for young people, like Camp X-treme, an annual six-day adventure blow-out in Texas.

If your family enjoys outdoor activities like fishing or hunting, with a little creativity (and maybe some advice from an adaptive outdoor recreation program), you can be included on most adventures.

Matt McLaughlin

Matt McLaughlin is a real outdoorsy guy. Matt, who is 8 years old, is an avid snow skier. He skis with his mom and another family. Since they live in Colorado, it's easy to pack up the car and head to one of the many ski parks. The families have also gone water skiing and river rafting. With Adaptive Adventures, Matt has tried rock climbing, played sled hockey and rugby, and learned how to handcycle.

But as much as he loves the great outdoors, Matt's favorite sport is played in a gym: wheelchair football. He says, "You can play with any amount of people. Offense needs more people than defense, so if you have an odd number of players, you put more on offense. You just improvise." Matt's goal is to organize a wheelchair football league and see the sport become more popular.

Matt has spinal muscular atrophy, which causes weak muscles. He has full sensation, but he can't walk. Last year he was the only wheelchair-user in his summer theater camp. For six weeks, campers learned about every aspect of putting on a show, then performed their original work at a theater in Denver.

Matt says the most important things are doing what you enjoy and having the confidence to try new things. "If I met a kid who used a wheelchair who wasn't very active," says Matt, "I would ask, What do you want to do? Because you can do anything you want, really. The main thing is feeling like you can do it. Then trying it."

profile

Photo courtesy of Challenge Aspen

Organized camps allow you to try many different sports in one setting.

Power Hockey

As the name implies, power hockey is played in power chairs. The game is played on a basketball court or in a gym, with lightweight plastic hockey sticks and a ball instead of a puck. Other than that, the sport (also called electric wheelchair hockey) follows the rules of ice hockey — only without the ice.

For players who can't hold a stick, a stick is bracketed onto the side of their chair. The player then passes, blocks and shoots by moving his or her chair.

Right now there aren't any junior teams in the United States, but kids can play on adult teams. There are six teams in Minnesota and one in Chicago. Teams are also developing in North Carolina, California, Pennsylvania and other places.

It's no surprise that Canada has many power hockey teams, especially in the Toronto area. So far Toronto has the only organized junior division, so if you're a power-chair-using Canadian, give them a call.

Power Soccer

Power soccer — also called indoor wheelchair soccer — is almost identical to stand-up soccer, except it's played in a gym and the players run around in electric chairs. Instead of using their feet, players kick and pass the ball with their chairs (with special footguards).

Anyone who uses a power chair can play. There aren't usually enough players to split up into adult and junior divisions, so everyone plays together.

Power soccer isn't available every-

where yet, but the sport is growing fast. If you live in Georgia, there are 14 power soccer teams (all juniors) in your state's adaptive sports program. Other big power soccer programs are at the Charlotte Rehab Institute in North Carolina, the Bennett Institute in Baltimore, and several programs in California. If you'd like to try the sport but don't live near any of these places, ask your local adaptive sports program or rehab hospital about forming a team.

Michael Timpa

R acing changes everything," says Michael Timpa. "It changes the way you look at the world. Once you get into it, you love it, and you don't want to stop. It becomes a way of life."

Michael discovered that way of life through GUMBO, Louisiana's statewide adaptive P.E. program, when he was 8. (GUMBO stands for Games Uniting Mind and Body.) Now Michael is 16, and competes in junior wheelchair competitions all over the country.

Michael does all the track events, from the 100- and 200-meter sprints, up to the 5,000- meter. During racing season he trains 2 to 2-1/2 hours every day, sometimes twice a day. Like a lot of young wheelchair athletes, Michael's coach is his dad. They learned about

ball, I fish, I ride my four-wheeler, I handcycle — I'll do anything I can get my hands on." Last summer Michael went to Camp X-treme in Texas, where he tried scuba diving, kayaking and rock climbing, along with slightly less extreme sports like basketball, football, softball, floor hockey and swimming.

Michael is now racing in his Eagle racing chair — he gave his first two to athletes who were just starting out. "First I loaned my chair to a kid in GUMBO," he says. "He looked like he could be a good racer — he had a good build for it, and he loved doing it, just like me. He trained a little bit, and he totally loved it, so I gave him the chair." Michael says proudly, "Since then he's been racing with it, and he's doing great."

Michael feels it's important to make those connections with other wheelchair athletes. "It helps you cope with a lot of things," he says. "Everyone is just like you. You might think you can't do something, but you see someone else doing it — so that means you can, too."

In the summer Michael runs the national races, and during the school year he still competes in GUMBO

role model

training by going to competitions, talking to people and asking questions — figuring it out as they went along.

Racing is Michael's first passion, but there's not a wheelchair sport he hasn't tried. "I play football, baseball, basket-

events. He holds the GUMBO Junior Division records for the 100 and 200 meters. Until he graduates, Michael wants to continue the GUMBO races, because, he says, "there are still records I haven't broken."

Racing

More than any other sport, wheelchair racing has shown the public what people in wheelchairs can do. Thanks to the activism and persistence of wheelchair athletes in the 1970s and '80s, city marathons all over the world now include a wheelchair division. Maybe you've seen these road warriors in their shiny suits and sleek chairs.

There are two kinds of wheelchair races: track and road. Track events are shorter and faster, like the 100 meter, 200 meter and 400 meter. For those, you need quick starts and bursts of strength. Road racing is for longer distances, like 5,000 or 10,000 kilometers ("Ks"), and marathons. Road racing requires endurance (staying power) *Continued on next page*

Sarah Marks

Sarah Marks has a theory about competition. "Training for track is tough," she says. "It involves pain. And the only reason you would want to do something painful is if you're good at it. So the first year I did it, I decided that I could win. And I won. So after that, I decided that I liked it."

Basketball, on the other hand, is more recreational for Sarah. She plays wheelchair basketball for the BORP Bay Cruisers. (BORP stands for Bay Area Outreach and Recreation Program.) She's been playing since she was 9, using one of BORP's chairs. "I've made a lot of friends at BORP," says Sarah. "The coaches' biggest object is for us to have fun. So it's not just exercise, it's social."

Sarah, now 14, saves her more serious training for racing. She has her own Quickie racing chair, and competes in the 100, 200, 400, 800 and 1500 meter events. She's been to the Junior Nationals three times, and plans to work hard and improve her speeds.

Sarah has spina bifida. She's not a full-time wheelchair user, but like a lot of kids, as she gets older, she's using her chair more and walking less. Also like a lot of families, Sarah's mom would prefer it the other way around. It's a bit of a battle for who decides.

Sarah has two cats, Spider and Nancy, and of course she also wants a dog. Besides racing, Sarah likes to hang out with her friends, read (especially "Harry Potter" books), and sometimes do stuff with her Girl Scout Troop.

Sarah has a lot of friends, some who have disabilities, some who don't. She feels both are important. A wheelchair sports program is important, too. She says, "For the whole day, once a week, you're with a whole group of people who are all the same, and they've all dealt with their own problems. That helps a lot."

profile

Racing (continued)

and good aerobic conditioning (strong heart and lungs).

Road racers also use techniques like "drafting" — following closely behind another racer, so he reduces your wind resistance and you conserve energy. On the track, everyone just pushes as hard as they can.

You can try racing in your everyday chair, but it's probably too heavy for competition. Racing chairs are very lightweight and designed to have less wind resistance.

Good racing chairs are expensive, but many adaptive sports programs have chairs you can use. Also, serious racers upgrade their chairs, so you might find a used chair at a good price.

Kids usually start at the track on shorter events. Most serious racers compete in road events like 5Ks, 10Ks and marathons all year, then train at the track for National Championships and other big events.

Rugby

To play on an official rugby team, you must be quadriplegic or a quadruple amputee. In fact, in the United States, the sport is known as "quad rugby." Because there aren't a lot of kids who are quads, quad rugby doesn't have an official junior division.

But the key word there is "official." Lots of adaptive sports programs and camps play rugby with people with all kinds of disabilities.

Why play rugby if you can't officially compete? Because the game is a blast!

Imagine a combination of football, soccer and bumper cars. The object of the game is to get the ball to the opposite end zone, similar to a touchdown in football. A line of defenders tries to stop you. And they try hard. Rugby is a full contact sport, so you don't want to play in your everyday chair.

If you *are* quadriplegic, rugby teams have no age restriction. Both girls and boys have played on quad rugby teams, and some of them are very good. To read about one of them, see the next page.

Skiing

Adaptive ski equipment allows you to ski sitting (background) or maybe standing in a "Ski-Legs" frame like the one at right.

Photograph by Michael Stoner

Some say the world is divided into two kinds of people: people who ski, and people who don't. If this is true, how will you know which you are until you try it?

Alpine (Downhill)

The most popular kind of snow skiing is downhill, or alpine, skiing. Downhill skiing is fast, exciting and not without danger. It comes complete with its own culture — clothing, equipment, pre- and

Continued on page 44

Nick Springer

Nick Springer plays — and loves — both sled hockey and quad rugby. He hopes he never has to choose between the two.

Nick is 18 years old. When he was 14, he had meningitis, a disease that affects the brain and spinal cord. Because of the illness, Nick had both his arms and both his legs amputated.

He was in the hospital for four months, and in rehab for another five months. A few months after that — about a year after getting sick — Nick started playing sled hockey. He immediately loved it, and when a teammate told him about rugby, he couldn't wait to start.

But Nick doesn't play on a junior teams — rugby doesn't have a youth division, and there are no junior sled hockey teams in his area. So Nick's teammates are all adults.

role model

Nick says being the youngest player on both the EPVA Jets (rugby) and the EPVA Islanders (hockey) has advantages and disadvantages. "Sometimes it's cool, because everyone thinks, he's young, he won't do much. Then they see what I can do and their jaws drop. Other times my entire team goes out to a bar and I get stuck back at the hotel."

Nick, who lives in Croton-on-Hudson, New York, has seen the benefits of sports again and again. "I know kids who, once they started playing disabled sports, their grades went up, they made more friends, they had more self-esteem. I've seen it happen." For himself, he says, "Sports helped me adapt. Through disabled sports, I've met a lot people who are in the same situation as me. It helped me get out there and do what I have to do."

Nick plans to go to college to study writing and film. He wants to find a college near a highly competitive rugby team. When teams heard he might be coming to their area, "their eyes lit up."

Although Nick was able-bodied until he was 14 years old, he says without hesitation: "Some of the best times of my life have been playing disabled sports."

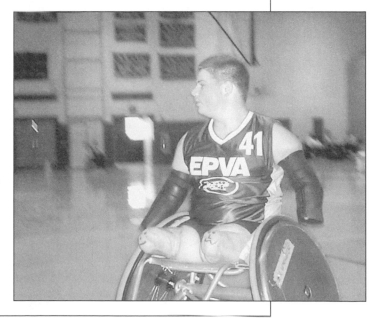

Skiing (continued)

post-ski rituals — which, for many people, is part of the attraction.

People who use wheelchairs ski pretty much the way anyone else does, except most do it sitting down. (If you can use a walker, you may be able to ski with equipment similar to a standing

Many sit-skiers start with a bi-ski (right) and move up to a monoski (below) when they develop advanced skills.

Photo courtesy of Mountain Photo, Snowmass

Photo by Amanda Boxtel

frame.) Sit-skis come in two varieties: the bi-ski and the monoski.

The bi-ski has outriggers on the side, to help with balance, stability and steering. It's better for beginners, and for people with less upper-body strength. When you're first learning, your bi-ski will be tethered (connected by a cord) to an experienced skier.

The monoski is for more advanced skiers. Monoskiers can become phenomenal skiers, conquering slopes and courses on a world-class level. But, like all sports, most people ski recreationally, not competitively. (Unless you count competing with your little brother.)

Nordic (Cross-country)

Nordic skiing, also called cross-country skiing, is a totally different experience. Where downhill is fast, Nordic is slow and steady. Where downhill calls for balance, quick reflexes and sheer nerve, Nordic requires arm strength, aerobic conditioning and perseverance. And where downhill skiing can be a very social event, full of people and parties, Nordic skiers enjoy the beauty of winter in peace and quiet.

Cross-country skiing for people with disabilities is less developed than its downhill cousin. There are some unique challenges, like the risk of becoming overheated. Working so hard while wearing winter clothes, especially in high altitudes, can be dangerous. But good instructors — and flat trails — help make it safe.

There are advantages, too. Unlike alpine skiing, you can learn some basic techniques and be gliding across a flat, straight, open stretch of snow in no time.

Water

Water skiers with disabilities also use

sit-skis (see photo, page 38). Many water-skiing centers have adapted equipment — and many adaptive sports programs include water-skiing among their summer options. It's fast, cold and wet: a great way to cool off on a sweltering day.

Skiing isn't possible for everyone. It involves travel and it can be expensive. But this is true whether or not you have a disability! Some adaptive ski programs — like Breckenridge, Winter Park and Maine Handicapped Skiing — are famous for their experienced instructors and excellent equipment. But many other ski resorts have good adaptive programs, too. Your family can compare rates for instruction, equipment rental and lift tickets, as well as travel time and costs.

Stacy Marx

role model

Ask Stacy Marx how she felt the first time she went snow skiing, and she makes the sign for "free."

Stacy is deaf and communicates through American Sign Language (ASL). She also emails and uses a "light talker" — a communication device that lets two people type to each other, with a computer speaking their words.

Stacy is 17 years old. She has cerebral palsy and uses a power chair. She plays on the Power CIRge, the power soccer team at the Charlotte Institute of Rehabilitation (CIR). Most power soccer players are adults, but the Power CIRge is almost all kids and teens. But their age doesn't hold them back: The CIRge placed second in their division in the 2003 national tournament.

When she plays soccer, Stacy has an extra challenge: she can't hear the referee's whistle and most refs don't sign. An assistant runs along the court to let Stacy know when a whistle has blown.

In addition to her weekly power soccer practice, Stacy rides horses. When she was 7 years old, Stacy was the first rider in the brand-new Misty Meadows Mitey Riders therapeutic riding program. Ten years later, the Mitey Riders is still a big part of Stacy's life — she never misses a week. Horseback riding has improved Stacy's balance, stability and muscle control. It's also helped her become a more independent, confident person.

During the summer, Stacy water-skis at Lake Norman, North Carolina. It's one of her favorite things to do. For two years, she took wheelchair dance classes, and she plays other sports, like tennis, just for fun.

Stacy is a junior at Mecklenburg High School. Last year she decided she wants to attend Gallaudet University, the famous college for people who are deaf or hearing-impaired. To achieve that goal, she'll have to focus hard on her academics, so Stacy decided to cut back on her after-school activities.

But not all of them. Riding got moved to Saturdays — and there's just no way she'll give up soccer. There are still championships to be won.

sports

Sled Hockey

Sled hockey is ice hockey without the skates. Players sit on short sleds that are raised slightly above the ice, and they use two short hockey sticks. The sticks serve two functions. They are used to pass and shoot the puck, of course. But the sticks also have picks at the end, something like the toe of a skate, and players use them to propel themselves across the ice.

Sled hockey is a fast, exciting, highly competitive game, and players are passionate about their sport. How passionate? Sled hockey is the only adaptive sport where all players wear helmets, face shields and lots of protective padding — and they need every bit of it.

Jesse Lawrence

Jesse Lawrence likes his sports fast, rough and very competitive. That's why he plays sled hockey.

Jesse's team, the Mighty Otters, practices twice a month at an ice rink near his home in Waterford, Pennsylvania. A few times a year, they travel to tournaments in Buffalo, Toronto, Baltimore and other cities. Tournament time is great — Jesse loves the travel and the competition. Last year the Mighty Otters represented western Pennsylvania at the Keystone Games, beating Eastern Pennsylvania to become state champs.

Jesse also plays wheelchair basketball, and he has tried parasailing and snow skiing. He sometimes plays street hockey with friends in his neighborhood — a wheelchair player can make a good goalie. On his sled hockey team, Jesse plays center. Jesse has a spinal cord injury, the result of a car accident when he was less than a year old.

In eighth grade at Fort LeBouef Middle School, Jesse likes school, especially math. He'll watch hockey on TV when the Buffalo Sabers are on, but he loves football — his team is the Pittsburgh Steelers. The Lawrence household could field a hockey team on its own: Jesse has one brother and three sisters.

Jesse hopes to play a lot more sled hockey, to practice hard and refine his skills. He hopes to one day play on the U.S. Paralympic team. That would be the ultimate goal.

Softball

Wheelchair softball is played on a hard surface instead of grass, so players can push their chairs around the bases and after balls. There are a few other wheelchair-only rules — for example, a player's legs cannot touch the ground. Other than that, it's basically the same sport as the stand-up game.

Lots of adapted sports camps organize wheelchair softball games, and everyone should give it a try. The National Wheelchair Softball Association docsn't have a junior division yet, but kids are welcome on adult teams.

Most major league baseball teams sponsor wheelchair softball teams. If you're a baseball fan, you might want to check out what your team is doing. The Chicago Cubs, Colorado Rockies, St. Louis Cardinals, Minnesota Twins and New York Mets all have big wheelchair softball programs. (That's not a complete list — go to your team's Web site and look under "community.")

Little League Baseball has a program for kids with disabilities called the "Challenger Division," but it's not true wheelchair sports. The Challengers mix kids with developmental disabilities, kids with physical disabilities and blind kids,

along with nondisabled players. Kids in chairs are paired with "baseball buddies" — nondisabled kids who push them around the bases. Most wheelchair sports coaches don't recommend it if you are a serious athlete, but it can be fun.

Since wheelchair softball is played on a hard surface, the ball moves fast. If you hit a ball to left field and you're busting it down the line to first base, don't be surprised if the ball gets there before you do.

Swimming

Swimming may just be the world's most perfect sport.

It gives you a great aerobic workout, strengthens your muscles and improves coordination — all without stressing your joints. It requires almost no equipment (unless you call a swimsuit and towel equipment). It's relaxing, soothing, refreshing and invigorating.

Most people, with or without disabilities, find swimming increases their range of motion and flexibility. If you'll

pardon the pun, swimming makes you more "fluid."

Finding a local pool that is accessible shouldn't be too difficult. Finding good lessons might be a little trickier. It's important to work with a swim instructor who understands how to adapt lessons for your disability. Many kids find one-on-one lessons much easier than group classes, but if it's a group of kids with disabilities, that will work, too.

sports

Sean Burns

Sean Burns is always doing something. He might be swimming at the local YMCA, practicing his archery in the back-yard, training on his stationary racing chair, riding his handcycle, or playing basketball with his team, the Buzzer Beaters, at the Charlotte Institute of Rehab. In the summer, there's water-skiing every week, and in the winter there's snow skiing in the Smoky Mountains. Sean has an older brother and four — yes, four — dogs, so there's usually someone to horse around with.

When Sean was 7 months old, he had transverse myelitis, a virus that damaged his spinal cord. Pretty much as soon as he got a wheelchair, he started playing sports. Sean is 9, and he's already been to four Junior Nationals. At the 2003 Nationals, Sean competed in track, field, archery and swimming.

Like most 9-year-old boys, Sean likes to hang out and play video games. But Sean takes his training seriously, and he likes to win. His goal is to race in the Paralympics, and he knows he has to work hard to get there.

Sean also likes to watch sports on TV. In the morning, he goes right to SportsCenter to check out the high-lights. His teams are the Braves (base-ball), the Hornets (basketball) and the Panthers (football). Sean's favorite spec-tator sport is baseball, but when asked who is favorite athlete is, he doesn't name Chipper Jones or Andruw Jones. Sean's favorite athlete is Dave Kiley.

You might not know Dave Kiley's name, but he is one of the superstars of wheelchair sports. Dave is the winner of *13* Paralympic medals, including three gold in basketball, two gold in skiing and four gold in track and field. A complete list of Kiley's accomplish-ments would take up the rest of this chapter, but here is one to appreciate: He was voted Most Valuable Player of the first *50 years* of wheelchair basket-ball.

And Dave Kiley just happens to be Sean Burns' basketball coach. The Charlotte Buzzer Beaters are one lucky team.

Sean has enjoyed every sport he's tried, and he'll probably play them all for a long time. But as he gets older, Sean plans to focus on track, to pursue his ultimate goal. Look for his name at a future Paralympic medal ceremony.

Table Tennis

Table tennis is easy to learn and easy to love. Table tennis is very popular at adapted sports camps, where kids barely tall enough to see above the table are pinging and ponging away.

If your family has room in the basement, you can set up a table and play against your parents, friends and siblings. If you live near an accessible rec center, you can play there. If you want to test your skills against serious players, Table Tennis USA — the people who govern the sport for competitive play — can tell you if there's a table tennis club in your area that uses a wheelchair-accessible center.

Wheelchair table tennis is also a Paralympic sport, played under the exact same rules as stand-up table tennis. On the competitive level, table tennis requires sharp eye-hand coordination and rapid-fire reflexes. But this sport doesn't have to be super-competitive to be fun.

Be warned. Once you pick up a paddle and challenge your friend to a game, she may call "two out of three." After that it's "best of seven", and before you know it, you're late for dinner.

Once you learn the basics, you can play against other wheelchair users or stand-up players.

Tennis

Tennis is perfect for wheelchair play. The rules are the same as stand-up tennis, except the wheelchair player is allowed two bounces of the ball. (The official wheelchair tennis newsletter is called *Two Bounce News*.)

Once you learn the basics, you can play against other wheelchair users or stand-up players. You can start in your everyday chair, or borrow a tennis chair from your local sports program. Tennis chairs are lighter, with cambered (angled) wheels, which make them easier to maneuver. There are also "all court" chairs that work for both basketball and tennis.

Wheelchair tennis is a very organized sport, with divisions for men, women, juniors and seniors, as well as different disability classifications. It's played all over the country, and anyone who can't run is eligible.

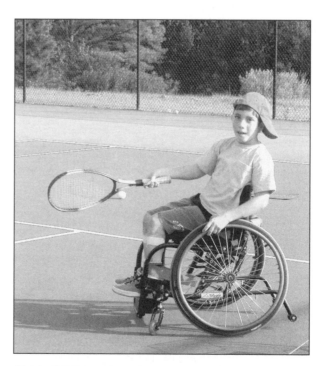

Keith Goldberg often plays wheelchair tennis with his twin brother, Todd. See their profile, page 16.

sports

Will Kirkpatrick

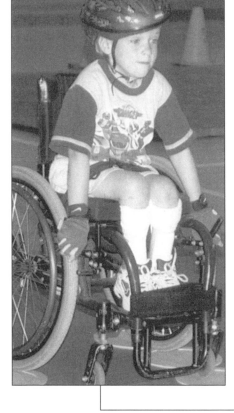

Y ou know that not everyone who uses a wheelchair plays sports. But did you know that not everyone who plays wheelchair sports uses a wheelchair?

Will Kirkpatrick is 7 years old and has spina bifida. His younger brother David does not have a disability. But at Super Sports Saturday at the Lakeshore Foundation, everyone gets in a chair to play. On most Saturdays, Will and David Kirkpatrick are racing, shooting, passing, blocking, volleying and whatever else, all from wheelchairs.

Will can't remember a time when he wasn't playing sports. It's no wonder, since he started swimming the day before his first birthday. He's been at the pool almost every week since then. At Lakeshore, in Birmingham, Alabama, Will has played a little bit of everything — wheelchair hockey, basketball, tennis, rugby. Will loves a game called "Shark," a wheelchair version of tag or capture the flag. Will says, "I'm great at it."

profile

Last year, Will started training for track with one of Lakeshore's racing chairs. His dad took him to his first competition, the Dixie Wheelchair Games in Georgia. Will says, "I did shotput, discus, track, softball and javelin. I did the 100, the 200 and the 400. I loved it. It was so fun. You get hot. But it's so fun."

Will also loves to watch sports, especially the Crimson Tide — University of Alabama football. Will went to a 'Bama football game with his uncle, and can't wait to do that again. Will says, "Almost my whole entire family are Alabama fans, except for my *brother* — he's an Auburn fan."

Tatyana and Hannah McFadden

Some people are gifted athletes. Some people use wheelchairs. Tatyana McFadden is both.

Tatyana is 14 years old. She lives in Clarksville, Maryland, and has spina bifida. Tatyana has been active in sports since she was 7, first swimming at a local pool, then going to the Bennett Institute in Baltimore every Saturday. At Bennett, Tatyana tried table tennis, archery, tennis, softball, football, skiing, and her two favorite sports, basketball and racing.

Over the years, Tatyana's pile of medals and trophies from the Junior Nationals and other tournaments has been steadily growing. Now the U.S. Paralympic track, basketball and sled hockey teams all want her to train for the 2004 Paralympics in Athens. She's decided to go for track, but she doesn't want to give up basketball.

When asked to predict future Paralympic stars, coaches all over the country mention her name. But Tatyana herself — though focussed and determined — is very low key. She says, "I just want to work hard and do well."

Training for the Paralympic track team will be anything but low-key. Tatyana will work out at the track three times a week. She'll also lift weights and use a roller (a racing chair that

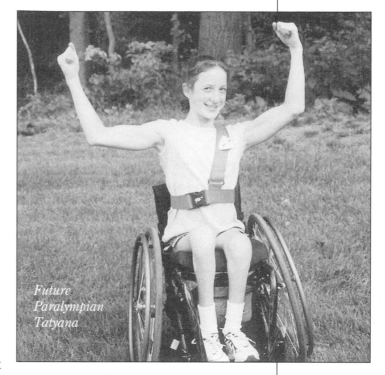

Future Paralympian Tatyana

stays in place like a treadmill) at home.

Hannah McFadden, Tatyana's younger sister, also plays sports at Bennett. Hannah was born without a hip joint and had her left leg amputated. Hannah walks with a prosthetic (an artificial leg), and she plays sports both on her crutches and using a wheelchair.

Hannah loves to swim, play wheelchair basketball and race. She loves meeting new friends at Bennett, but she's not convinced she wants to compete like her sister. Hannah ran her first race when she was 4 years old — all the kids got medals. Hannah's coach said, "Come on, let's run another race!"

Hannah asked, "Why?"

Her coach said, "You'll get another medal."

Hannah looked down at the medal in her hand and said, "Got one. Don't need another."

Hannah likes playing more than competing.

Resources

We don't have room to list every adaptive sports organization in the country. So if you don't see one here that is near you, don't worry! You can do a "Google" Internet search for programs in your area, or look up the links on the sites listed here.

Start Here

• Adaptive Adventures, P.O. Box 2245 Evergreen, CO 80437; 877-679-2770; 303-679-2770; Chicago Office: Chicago, 230 Greenleaf Ave. Wilmette, IL 60091; 866-679-2770; 847-251-8445; www.adaptivead ventures.org. This Web site has great listings by state and by sport. Look here first!

• National Center on Physical Activity and Disability, 1640 W. Roosevelt Rd., Chicago, IL 60608; 800-900-8086; www.ncpad.org. Excellent database.

• Sports 'n Spokes Directory of Wheelchair Sports Associations, PVA Publications, 2111 E. Highland Ave., Suite 180 , Phoenix, AZ 85016; 888-888-2201; 602-224-0500; www.sns-magazine.com/sns/wheelcha.htm

Selected Programs

• Adaptive Sports Center of Crested Butte, PO Box 1639, Crested Butte, CO 81224; 866-349-2296; 970-349-2296; www.adaptivesports.org

• Adaptive Sports in New York City and State, Windham Mountain CD Lane Rd., Windham, NY 12496; 518-734-5070; www.nyc.gov/html/sports/ html/cityandstate-adaptive.html

• Austin Adaptive Sports Center, 100 E. 41st St., Suite 965, Austin, TX 78751; 512-451-3637; www.austinadaptive sports.com

• Blaze Sports, U.S. Disabled Athletes Fund, 280 Interstate North Circle, Suite 450, Atlanta, GA 30339; 770-850-8199; www.blazesports.com

• BORP: Bay Area Outreach and Recreation Program, 3210 Tolman Hall, MC 1650, Berkeley, CA 94720; 510-643-0131; www.borp.org

• Breckenridge Outdoor Education Center, PO Box 697, Breckenridge, CO 80424; 970-453-6422; www.boec.org

• Challenge Aspen, P.O. Box M, Aspen, CO 81612; 970-923-0578; www. challengeaspen.com

• City of San Jose, Office of Therapeutic Services, San Jose, CA 95101; 408-392-6700; www.ci.san-jose.ca.us/prns/ rcsots.htm

• Courage Center, 3915 Golden Valley Road, Minneapolis, MN 55422; 888-8INTAKE; 763-520-0312; www. courage.org

• EPVA: Eastern Paralyzed Veterans Association, 75-20 Astoria Blvd., Jackson Heights, NY 11370; 718-803-3782; www.epva.org

• Great Lakes Adaptive Sports Association (GLASA), 400 E. Illinois Road, Lake Forest, IL 60045; 847-283-0908; http://home.wi.rr.com/glasa

• Lakeshore Foundation, 4000 Ridgeway Dr., Birmingham, AL 35209; 205-313-7400; www.lakeshore.org

• Maine Handicapped Skiing (more than skiing), Sunday River Ski Resort, 8 Sundance Lane , Newry, ME 04261; 800-639-7770; 207-824-2440; www.skimhs.org

• National Abilities Center, PO Box 682799, Park City, UT 84068; 435-649-3991; www.nac1985.org

• National Sports Center for the Disabled, P.O. Box 1290, Winter Park,

Colorado 80482; 970-726-1540; 303-316-1540; Denver Office: 633 17th Street, #24, Denver, CO 80202; 303-293-5711; www.nscd.org

• Shake-A-Leg (sailing), 200 Harrison Ave. Newport, RI 02840; 401-846-5545; www.shakealeg.org

Selected Programs: Rehab Centers

• ASAP: Adaptive Sports Adventure Program at Charlotte Institute of Rehabilitation, PO Box 32861, Charlotte, NC 28232; 704-355-2000; www.carolinas.org

• Bennett Institute, 707 N. Broadway, Baltimore, MD 21205; 800-873-3377; 443-923-9200; www.kennedykrieger.org

• Casa Colina, 255 E. Bonita Ave., PO Box 6001, Pomona, CA 91769-6001; 800-926-5462; 909-596-7733; www.casa colina.org

• CHAMPS: Cleveland Clinic Children's Hospital For Rehabilitation, 2801 Martin Luther King Jr. Dr., Cleveland, OH 44104; 216-721-5400; www.cleveland clinic.org

• Massachusetts Hospital School, 3 Randolph St., Canton, MA 02021; 781-828-2440; www.mass.gov

• RIC: Rehabilitation Institute of Chicago, 345 E. Superior, Suite 1408, Chicago, IL 60611; 800-354- 7342; 312-238-6066; www.ric.org

• Shepherd Center, 2020 Peachtree Rd. NW, Atlanta, GA 30309; 404-367-1378; www.shepherd.org

Governing Orgs.

• National Disability Sports Alliance (formerly US Cerebral Palsy Athletic Association), 25 W. Independence Way, Kingston, RI 02881; 407-792-7130;

Find a Camp

Camp is a great way to experience new activities. There are three basic kinds of camp: general camps that welcome all kids; "special needs" camps designed for access that are able to handle personal care or even medical treatment; and adaptive sports camps. To locate an adaptive sports camp, check with the organizations on this page. For the  other two kinds of camps, check this Web site: http://find.acacamps.org/finding_special_needs.htm

Camp X-treme

Camp X-treme is for independent kids 10 and up. For six days, kids with physical disabilities explore their potential and try things they thought were impossible. The extreme sports activities are taught by world-class wheelchair athletes and other experts. For info, call 210-592-5358. This camp is sponsored by three Texas rehab hospitals, with a Web page on the Warm Springs site at www.warmsprings.org.

www.ndsaonline.org

• National Wheelchair Basketball Association, 6917 Grand Prarie Dr., Colorado Springs, CO; 719-266-4082; www.nwba.org

• Wheelchair Sports USA, 10 Lake Circle Suite G19, Colorado Springs, CO 80906; 719-574-1150; www.wsusa.org 🦿

LAURA KAMINKER has been writing about the wheeling life since 1988, with a special interest in wheelchair sports. Her work has appeared in Sports Illustrated for Kids, Seventeen, Newsweek *and* The New York Times, *among other places. She is also the author of several books and educational videos for teenagers. Laura lives in New York City with Allan Wood, who is also a writer, and their two wonderful dogs. Readers are invited to email Laura at landa@earthlink.net.*

fun and games

*By Jean Dobbs
& Matt Meyers*

Just For the Fun of It!

The best part of being a kid is that you get to play a lot. You make up stories, invent games, and generally do things just for the fun of it. You even have places built for playing — treehouses and playgrounds.

In the past, kids with disabilities weren't always included in fun and games, but these days, there are accessible structures, adaptive video game controls, dolls with disabilities and other toys that keep in mind kids on wheels.

Photo courtesy of Landscape Structures

Accessible playgrounds are popping up all over the country.

A Ramp to the Trees

Chaz Freeman is very active. He hosts a talk show at his school, writes music (rap songs), and contributes to the newspaper and yearbook. But one of his favorite projects at Crotched Mountain School has been giving advice to the builders of an accessible treehouse.

"It makes me feel good," says Chaz, who has cerebral palsy. (He switches back and forth between manual and power chairs.)

"The more accessible treehouses there are, the more people are going to want to get out do recreational activities. They won't say, 'I can't do this, I'm not like the other kids.'"

In nice weather, the students will have campouts in the treehouse, which can hold three kids in power chairs or four in manual chairs.

Chaz

There are actually a few accessible treehouses around the country. If you look at the Web site www.treehouses.org, you can see photos and articles about other projects. Different challenges come up with each individual treehouse.

For example, one thing the builders at Crotched Mountain didn't think about is that in New Hampshire there are wild turkeys looking for shelter. At first there was no door on the treehouse. "We had turkeys in the treehouse, so then we really had to put a lock on," Chaz says. The kids are considering a sign for the door: "No Turkeys Allowed!"

Photo courtesy of Crotched Mountain School

Barrier-Free Playgrounds

A more common accessible structure is a new kind of playground that is popping up all over the country. The idea is to use "universal design," which basically means that all kids can play on the structures, whether they have disabilities or not.

Some of these playgrounds have waist-high sand tables instead of sandboxes on the ground (your wheelchair fits under the table). Some structures have a ramp up to a raised cabin. In general, all the spaces in or between equipment are wide enough for wheelchairs.

A great organization that helps schools and parks build accessible structures is called Boundless Playgrounds. Their Web site also lists places that already have them — see if your city does by going to the Web site www.boundlessplaygrounds.org. If your school or local park is building new equipment, make sure the project leaders know about this resource. By sharing this information, you can make a difference in your community!

Photo courtesy of Landscape Structures

Halloween on Wheels

A lot of kids who use wheelchairs have a blast at Halloween. Instead of buying costumes from a store, their parents help them make something cool that works well on wheels.

Clay, who has cerebral palsy, is 16 now, but he and his family have been designing great costumes since he was 5. People were so impressed with them that Clay's mom put the instructions on the Web site of Clay's elementary school (www.bridgeschool.org). She was also nice enough to send 11 years of photos to *Kids on Wheels* — they are spread over the next few pages.

Clay is mostly nonverbal, so he uses a few different ways to talk, including a voice output communication device. He answered questions for *Kids on Wheels* with a more low-tech method called "live voice scanning": Clay's Mom and a therapist gave him lots of word choices, and he said yes or no to pick the words he wanted.

"My sister and I have always had fun making wild costumes," Clay says. "Now people look forward to what I am going to be each year." What's his favorite? "It is hard to pick one favorite costume because each year I pick a character that is my favorite then." He adds that the Biker was one of the most fun because it was a big hit at school. "The other kids thought my Biker costume was so cool," Clay remembers. "I won best all around costume in eighth grade and my first year in high school for that one."

Continued on page 58

From Aladdin to Alligator Wrestler ...

Clay's Costumes

1. King Clay, age 5
2. Cowpoke, age 6
3. Aladdin, age 7
4. Superman, age 8
5. George of the Jungle, age 9
6. Punk Rock Drummer,
   ages 10 and 11

7. Shark-Bitten Surfer, age 12
8. Crocodile Hunter, age 13
9. Biker and Babe, ages 14
   and 15
10. Dr. Frankenstein and
    Frankenstein, age 16

and Beyond!

For color photos and costume instructions, go to www.bridgeschool.org

Jake uses wheels to his advantage with the Biker costume.

Trick-or-Treat!

Halloween just wouldn't be Halloween without candy. But sometimes it's hard to trick-or-treat in your own neighborhood because lots of houses have steps or narrow walkways. Sean likes to trick-or-treat at his dad's office because it's wheelchair-accessible, and that gives him more independence. He likes trick-or-treating in the neighborhood so he can see all the decorations, but "it is easier at Dad's work because there aren't any hills and sidewalks." If your parents work in places that are easy for you to get around in, ask them if they can start inviting kids there for Halloween.

If you are wheeling around the neighborhood and you have to wait at the bottom of steps, you can ask your friends to get you some candy, but it's even more fun if you invite your neighbors to come down and see your costume. Then you can pick out your own candy, too!

Maybe some of your neighbors

Last year, Jake Watson, who is 5 years old and has spina bifida, followed the instructions for the Biker on the Bridge School Web site. He got a lot of compliments, too. The year before, he did the King costume, and the year before that he was a Race Car Driver. What does Jake like most about Halloween? "Candy!" He also loves the fact that other kids like his costume. "They wish they could have a wheelchair, too," he says.

Although creating a costume is lots of fun, you can still have a great time in a store-bought outfit. Sean Grady, who is 8 and has spina bifida, wore a homemade Tiger costume one year, but last year he wanted to be Batman, so he got a packaged costume. Another idea is to modify — change — a store-bought costume to make it work better with your wheelchair. "It was a little hard to spread my bat wings," Sean says. If he goes as Batman again, he says a cape would work better than wings.

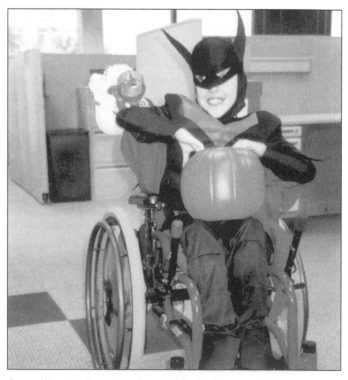

Sean likes trick-or-treating at his dad's accessible office.

already have a ramp for you because you come over to play all the time. If they do, ask your parents to remind them to put it out for you on Halloween — then you can get right up to the door.

Safety First

You probably already know that you shouldn't take candy from strangers, but there are some other dangerous things about Halloween that you should be aware of.

First, if you are making your own costume, always do it with your parents or another grownup. The tools or materials could hurt you if you try to do it alone. Have your parents check to make sure the materials are nontoxic — meaning they aren't poisonous.

Also, make sure your costume won't get caught in your wheels or cover your joystick - you need to be able to move freely. Likewise, you or your parents should be able to get you out of your chair easily, so watch out for costumes that strap you in too much.

Carving pumpkins can also be dangerous, especially if your hands don't work too well. If your parents say you can carve a pumpkin, always do it with them nearby. But if your disability affects your hands, leave the knives in the drawer! You can still describe or draw a Jack-o-lantern design and have Mom or Dad do the actual cutting.

Toys and Games

For years toy makers have made games and dolls that don't look like real people. Have you ever seen a doll or action figure with a pimple or one that is having a "bad hair day"? You probably haven't, and for a very long time it was the same for wheelchairs.

Over the past 10 years toy makers have gone from making no toys involving wheelchairs to now having quite a few. Of course, just because you use a wheelchair doesn't mean you have to play with toys and games with wheelchairs, but it is nice to know that you are included.

Barbie's friend Share-a-Smile Becky later became Photographer Becky.

Dolls

When we think about dolls, probably the first name that pops into our heads is Barbie. It may be tough to tell by looking at her flawless face, but Barbie is almost 45 years old! Even at her age, Barbie is extremely young in comparison to the length of time people have been making dolls.

Scientists believe that dolls have been around for 10,000 years or maybe longer.

In America, almost all doll makers made White dolls with blond hair and blue eyes. For years, many Black children felt like there was something wrong with them because there were no dolls that looked like them. The same thing was happening to kids with disabilities, but recently this has changed.

The first major company to make dolls in wheelchairs was Mattel. In 1996, they introduced a wheelchair as an accessory for their American Girls dolls. In that same year they introduced "Share-A-Smile Becky," Barbie's wheelchair-using friend. Becky was one of the most popular in Barbie's history, but Mattel accidentally did not make Becky's wheelchair fit inside Barbie's Dream House.

By the year 2000, the Mattel Company decided to redesign Becky in honor of the 2000 Paralympic Games. In the new design, Becky wore a blue and white uniform while sitting on a specially designed wheelchair for track races, she even comes with a patriotic red, white and blue helmet to protect her from injury.

Sara Schmidt, a 9-year-old wheelchair user and Barbie collector says, "It makes me happy that they have dolls like regular people."

Action Figures

Aidan Assist

Even more recently, Mattel has introduced the "Aidan Assist" action figure from Fisher Price's "Rescue Hero" series. Aidan, dressed in his paramedic uniform, has a wheelchair, equipped with flashing lights and an x-ray machine that lets him see if anyone has broken bones that he can help to mend.

Since the mid-1990s when Mattel began making wheelchair-using dolls, other companies began doing the same by making toys with all sorts of disabilities. An Internet company called Bindependent (www.bindependent.com) sells a set of dolls that have everything

Valerria Gordon: A Girl's Girl

"I Enjoy Being a Girl" is a song Valerria Gordon can relate to.

The 7-year-old loves nothing more than to play with her dolls — "I must have 1,000," she says — both Barbie dolls and baby dolls. She had one doll that used a wheelchair. It must be buried

under all the others, though, because she hasn't seen it in awhile!

Valerria, who has spina bifida, also loves to dress up, draw and color. She has a special bond with her 8-year-old brother, Robbie, who also has spina bifida. She and Robbie both have handcycles that they ride on the sidewalk outside their house in St. Petersburg, Florida. "We pedal with our hands — it's fun," she says.

Valerria is in the second grade at Tyrone Elementary School. Her favorite book is *The Lion and the Mouse*. Her favorite part of the day is recess, when she plays with all her friends. She and Robbie are also in the choir and a mime group at their church.

Valerria and Robbie have a big sister named Omarra, who is 16. "Robbie likes a lot of sports and Valerria is the girly-girl," Omarra says.

"When I found out my ma was pregnant again, I prayed and prayed that she would have a little girl because I always wanted a little sister. It was meant to be."

—By Carolyn Said

from leg braces to wheelchairs.

Recently, television and movies have had more characters with disabilities. The best example of this is probably "Professor X" from the *X-Men* comic books along with the film "X-Men" and "X2." Because of the popularity of these films, the Toy Biz Company has made action figures of Professor X in his futuristic wheelchair. The figurine is about six inches tall and there are two models.

The Oracle from the show "Birds of Prey" has also recently been molded into plastic. The Oracle, in her wheelchair, wears a green shirt and jeans. It may be a little more difficult finding The Oracle, as the maker of this toy only sells this figure directly to comic book stores. The Professor X figure, however, is available in most toy stores. Even though it may be "nice that Professor X is in a wheelchair," according to 11-year-old Patrick McGinley, "in the cartoon and in the movie, Professor X doesn't have the same problems that people like me do."

Some things change more slowly than others, and unfortunately making dolls and action figures with disabilities has taken a while. But it seems like the pace is picking up. It was only a couple of years ago that there were none. Hopefully, this is just the beginning of companies making dolls that look the way that people *really* look and don't just have the flawless face of Barbie.

Hard to Find Dolls

Share-a-Smile Becky is no longer being made, but you can get one on auction sites like www.ebay.com as Barbie collectibles. The regular models of Becky go for around $15-25 while the Paralympic Barbie sells for a few dollars more. Action figures like Aidan Assist and Professor X can also be found this way for about $10.

Doll and Action Figure Resources

These companies sell dolls with disabilities or adaptive equipment for dolls. If you can't find what you're looking for on the Web site, try putting in the word "wheelchair" in the "Search" box.

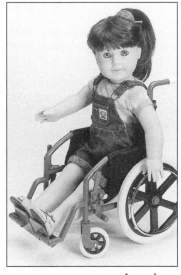

American Girl

- **Special Abilities**
P.O. Box 360, Wakefield
WF2 8WG
www.abilities.fsnet.co.uk/
toys/toys.html
- **Bindependant**
905 Warren Way,
Richardson TX 75080
www.bindependent.com
- **American Girl**
800-845-0005
www.americangirlstore.com
- **Lakeshore Learning Material**
800-243-5354
2695 Dominguez Ave., Carson CA 90810
www.lakeshorelearning.com
- **Fisher Price**
800-432-KIDS
www.fisher-price
(Toy bus with wheelchair access)
- **Bill Bam's Collectiables**
(209)551-4097
1613 Candler Lane, Mosesto CA 95355
www.billbam.com
(Professor X action figure; Sometimes they have Barbie's friend Becky)
- **Kaplan Early Learning Co.**
800-334-2014.
www.kaplanco.com
- **Creative Academics**
www.creativeacademics.com
- **Beyond Play**
1442-A Walnut Street #52,
Berkeley CA 94709
www.beyondplay.com/ITEMS/D899.HTM

Video Games

When you think about a superhero in a video game, do you ever think of someone in a wheelchair? Probably not. Some of the most popular games in the past few years have been ones with flying dragons, giant gorillas and people with supernatural powers as the heroes.

The first video game to have a wheelchair using character in an important role was 1993's "X-Men" for Sega Genesis. Unfortunately, it was almost 10 years until there was another game that had a wheelchair user as a prominent character.

In November of 2001, Microsoft introduced a new game for their X-Box game system called "Oddworld: Munch's Oddysee." Munch, a Gabbit (a made-up creature often hunted for their useful skin) lost one of his legs in a trap and was captured by an evil scientist. Eventually Munch escapes and discovers that while he was in the clutches of the evil scientist all but one of his fellow Gabbit's have been killed. It becomes

A Gabbit to the rescue!

Munch's mission to rescue his fellow Gabbit from a scientific research facility while there is still a chance for the Gabbit race to survive. Even though Munch is in a wheelchair due to the trapping incident, this never deters him from his mission.

Shortly after the release of "Munch," ARUSH Entertainment unveiled the new online game for PCs called "Monkey Brains." In this game, Dr. Simius (a wheelchair user) and Dr. Kreep have been sent to an island to perform research on how the human brain works. While performing experiments, Dr. Kreep discovers a machine that can control minds. It is the job of the monkeys along with Dr. Simius to stop Dr. Kreep before he leaves the island and brings his discovery back to the rest of the world. Rather than a computer game that you buy in a store and then load onto your PC, "Monkey Brains" is a game that you purchase online one episode at a time (there are a total of seven). ARUSH offers the first level as a free demo at www.arushgames.com/games/monkey brains and additional levels are sold for $5, or they allow you to buy the whole game for $19.99.

Acclaim Entertainment also recently released a game for PlayStation 2 called "Shadow Man: 2econd Coming" in which the story is based on the experiences of a former New York City police officer, Thomas Deacon, who uses a wheelchair.

Adaptive controllers allow you to play video games even if you can't use your hands.

In addition, Acclaim will be releasing another game entitled "Killer7" for Nintendo Gamecube in mid-2004. The hero is a wheelchair user with seven personalities.

Adaptive Controllers

Today there are several companies that make all sorts of adaptive controls to allow almost every wheelchair user to play the same games as non-wheelchair users.

One company, called KY Enterprises, makes a joystick controller that can even be operated by a sip-and-puff switch. Note: It can't be used with "analog" games, so check the boxes of your games. For more info, see www.quad control.com. If you have some hand function, you might try the Quad Commander instead (www.gpk.com).

Enabling Devices (www.enabling devices.com) is a company devoted to making life easier for wheelchair users. They not only sell things like computer mice that can be controlled by the direction of your head, but they are also willing to build one-of-a-kind devices for a specific person.

Glenn Burgess-Dennis is an 11-year-old with a spinal injury who is able to play almost all PlayStation and PS2 games with an extra-large controller. Too bad for his brother, Max. "It was hard to use when I got it, but now I kick Max's butt!" says Glenn, laughing. According to Glenn's mom, the controller made by Enabling Devices is one of the best things to happen to the family. "It's lets everyone play together, the whole family. And neither of the kids seems to feel neglected anymore."

Resources

These companies sell controls that allow kids with disabilities to play video games as well as anyone else. Some, like Access to Recreation, offer tons of products for having fun. Check them out!

- **Access to Recreation**
800-634-4351; www.accesstr.com
- **Enabling Devices**
800-832-869; www.enablingdevices.com
- **GPK**
800-468-8679; www.gpk.com
(Makes QuadCommander)
- **Pathways Development Group**
877-742-4604; www.pathwaysdg.com
(Adaptive controllers for Nintendo, Super NES & N64)
- **KY Enterprises**
562-433-5244; www.quadcontrol.com
(Adaptive joysticks and sip-and-puff controllers for PS1 & PS2)

Last Laugh

Someone once said, "Smile, and the world smiles with you." It's true! If you can laugh at life, so will your friends, family and neighbors!

animals

By Jean Dobbs

More Than Pets

If you or your friends have pets, you already know how much fun animals can be. But you may not know about *service animals* or *animal therapy*. And did you know there are *pets with disabilities*? Yes, there are dogs and cats that use wheelchairs!

Service Animals

Julia Grace Collins was a little nervous when she brought home her service dog, Jaan (sounds like "John"). Even *pet* dogs are a lot of work, and *service* dogs need extra training every day. But now she is really glad to have Jaan, because he helps her do more things without asking her mom for help. "He picks up things like pencils or erasers — just basically anything I drop," she says. "He opens drawers for me." (See Julia Grace's whole story on page 70.)

Service dogs usually help their owners by picking up dropped items, turning switches on or off, and doing other physical tasks. Also called "assistance dogs," these animals are trained for about two years to respond to dozens of commands. They might tow your chair or even pick up the phone when it rings — they are very smart dogs.

There are several organizations that train service dogs. One organization, Loving Paws Assistance Dogs, trains dogs just for children. They have two

Photo by Susan Collins

kinds of dogs — service dogs and "social dogs." Social dogs are for kids over 7 and are meant to be your "best friend and part-time helper." Service dogs are for kids over 12.

Another service dog organization, Canine Partners for Life, trains mostly golden retrievers and Labradors, or a cross of both. But they have trained Dobermans, greyhounds, setters and many other breeds — even poodles. By the time they are 2 or 2 1/2 years old, the dogs know as many as 40 commands and are ready to be placed with their new owners, also called "handlers."

Julia Grace and Jaan love their new life together.

Benjamin and Riley

"I wanted a service dog to help me with my independence."

—Benjamin Snow

Benjamin Snow, who is 16 and has cerebral palsy, recently went through the program and was matched with a Lab named Riley. Before he could bring her home to Denver, Colorado, he had to spend three weeks training with her at the Canine Partners for Life school in Pennsylvania. That was a year after he first applied and sent the organization a videotaped interview telling them his plans.

"The main reason I wanted a service dog was to help me with my independence," Benjamin says. "I've planned to go to college and live in a dorm room, so I figured Riley could help me by retrieving things" like books, pencils or clothes.

Now that Riley is home with

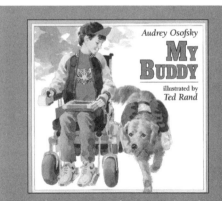

To learn more about service dogs, read *My Buddy*, a book about a kid with muscular dystrophy who gets an assistance dog (see review, page 97).

Benjamin, they train for half an hour or an hour every day. This way, Riley keeps fine-tuning her skills and learns new ones, too. In one month, she has learned the words "shoe," "buckle," and "sock." Now, when Benjamin tells her to "tug" these things, Riley pulls off his shoes and socks.

Some organizations train and place the dogs for free or a small fee, but there is usually a long waiting list at those places. If you think a service dog could help you be more independent, talk to your parents about getting on a list now. It could take a few years after you turn in an application, so you really need to plan ahead.

You should know that not everyone who applies gets a service dog. To increase your chances, be very clear in your application about how a dog could help you achieve your goals and live more independently.

If you do get matched with a dog and survive the training camp, there are lots of rules to follow when you get home. To keep service dogs doing the best job they can, they should not be treated as pets. For example, you should not let your friends pet them or give them commands — they should respond only to you. People understand this better if the dog wears a harness or backpack that says they are working dogs.

There is also the danger of relying on your dog too much. "There are some times when you could do things yourself," Benjamin says. "Don't think that just because you have a service dog that they will help you with everything. They help you with your independence. At the same time, it's part of your job to be the one who's independent."

Another animal that is sometimes trained to help adults with disabilities is the capuchin monkey. You don't see helper monkeys very often, but there are about 70 quadriplegics in the United States who have them. They are great because they have hands and can be trained to do things like feed their owners. Plus capuchin monkeys live for 35 to 45 years, so they can help for a long time! You can't have one as a kid, but if you have quadriplegia, you might qualify for one as an adult. To learn more, see the Helping Hands Web site: www.helpinghandsmonkeys.org.

Caitlin says, "I always have fun when I ride."

Hippotherapy

You may not like therapy when it's physical therapy or speech therapy, but "hippotherapy" is different. Don't worry — there are no hippos involved! "Hippo" comes from the Greek word for horse, and hippotherapy basically means horseback riding for health reasons.

The reason it's called "therapy" is because horseback riding improves muscle tone, balance, posture, coordination and motor development. But if you try it, it probably won't feel like work at all. "It doesn't feel like therapy because I always have fun when I ride a horse," says Caitlin McDermott, who is 10 and has spina bifida (see her profile in Chapter 1).

Horseback riding gently moves the rider's body in a way similar to the way the human body moves when walking. So even if you're a full-time wheelchair user, your body can feel as if you've walked around the block after you've ridden a horse around a ring. "Riding horses helps my balance and probably stretches out my legs because I'm not in that kind of position a lot," Caitlin explains.

In addition to riding, you may learn grooming and more advanced skills like trotting or even "vaulting" — jumping objects while on the horse.

But the best part is moving the same way as all riders. "I feel good when I

Service Dog Resources

• Assistance Dogs International, P.O. Box 110, Skippack, PA 19747; info@assistance-dogs-intl.org; www.assistance-dogs-intl.org
• Canine Companions for Independence, P.O. Box 446, Santa Rosa, CA 95402; 800-572-2275; www.caninecompanions.org
• Canine Partners for Life, P.O. Box 170, Cochranville, PA 19330-0170; www.k94life.org
• Loving Paws Assistance Dogs, P.O. Box 12005, Santa Rosa, CA 95406; www.lovingpaws.com
• International Association of Assistance Dog Partners; 38691 Filly Drive, Sterling Heights, MI 48310; www.iaadp.org
• Paws with a Cause, 4646 South Division, Wayland, MI 49348; 800/253-7297; www.pawswithacause.org

animals

Julia Grace Collins: Girl on the Go

Julia Grace Collins really gets around. Whether it's in her wheelchair, on her handcycle or on her scooter, Julia Grace likes to be independent, and she likes to be moving.

One of her favorite ways to move is by horse. Julia Grace, who is 9, has been horseback riding since she was 2. At first, she was afraid of the horses, but she stuck with it. Now, she says, "I go every week. I love it. You do exercises and have fun, and meet people, and the horses are so nice."

Julia Grace's scooter comes in handy at the riding center. The ground is sandy and uneven, making it hard to push a wheelchair. She also uses the scooter for longer distances, like trick-or-treating on Halloween, or visiting a friend in the neighborhood. In school, Julia Grace uses her wheelchair, though in the classroom she walks with her crutches. Julia Grace, who has spina bifida, can transfer independently between her different forms of transport.

Julia Grace recently took another step toward independence: She got an assistance dog. His name is Jaan (pronounced "John"), and he is mostly a golden retriever. Jaan is specially trained to do things like open doors, pick things up and turn on a light switch.

Adopting Jaan was a very long process. Julia Grace and her mom did a lot of research and filled out a lot of forms. After a long interview on the phone, they traveled from their home in North Carolina to Florida for another interview. Then they were put on a waiting list, until finally, they went back to Florida for two weeks of training.

In training, Julia Grace says, "We were doing things all day long. Sometimes it was like school, in a class. Other times we practiced with the dogs. Later, you get to have the dog in your room, and you take him to the mall. The teacher watches you and corrects your mistakes." Julia Grace found the training fun, difficult, tiring and exciting.

Julia Grace loves Jaan, but she also feels the weight of a big responsibility. "There are so many things to remember," she says. "Sometimes I worry that I won't be able to take care of him." Luckily for both dog and girl, her mom helps care for Jaan, too.

Like a lot of kids, Julia Grace sets very high standards for herself, and she feels upset if she doesn't achieve her goals. For example, if she gets a report card with all As and one B, she'll be angry about the B — even though a B is a very good grade! "I want to do everything right, but sometimes it just doesn't go that way," she says.

Julia Grace also doesn't like when friends or classmates try to help her too much. "I already have a helper at school, and she helps me when I ask her to," she says. "But if one of the other children tries to help me, then all of a sudden everybody wants to help. I don't like having so much attention just because of my wheelchair."

When she's not riding horses, tooling around on her handcycle or practicing lessons with Jaan, you might find Julia Grace in Junior Girl Scouts, or writing a story, or enjoying a good book. Or swimming. Or maybe she'll be trying something completely new.

— *By Laura Kaminker*

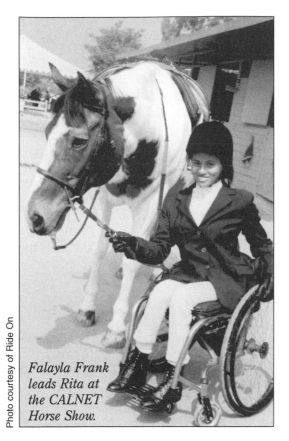

Falayla Frank leads Rita at the CALNET Horse Show.

Rachel Rassmussen: Building Confidence

Every Friday afternoon, Rachel Rasmussen rides horses at the National Abilities Center in Park City, Utah.

Rachel is 7 years old, but she started riding when she was only 4. Assistants — called "walkers" — would stand on each side, and another walker would lead the horse around the ring. Rachel would sit on the horse and do different stretching exercises. This increased Rachel's balance and strength — and her confidence.

Now Rachel, who has spina bifida, rides a horse without any side walkers. She sits straight in the saddle, holds the reins herself and gives the horse commands. The instructors place cones around the arena, and Rachel guides the horse around them.

When she gets to the stable, Rachel helps groom her horse — combing and brushing it, cleaning its hooves and conditioning its coat. She helps connect the saddle and reins, then walks the horse into the arena.

The horse is led to the side of a ramp. Instructors roll Rachel up the ramp, then lift her out of her wheelchair and onto the horse. Rachel was never afraid of the horses, but trusting the people who lifted her took a little getting used to.

— By Laura Kaminker

ride a horse because I'm high up and it lets me do what other kids are doing," says Caitlin. "It makes me feel like I'm a regular kid."

Resources:

• North American Riding for the Handicapped Association, 800-369-7433; www.narha.org.

• Ride On Therapeutic Horsemanship, 21126 Chatsworth St., Chatsworth, CA 91311; wwwRideOn.org

Pets on Wheels

Just like disabilities are a natural part of the human experience, paralysis happens to animals too. Good thing there are wheelchairs for them!

One company makes adaptive equipment for canines called K-9 Carts. But they're not just for dogs — these wheelchair-like devices can be used by cats or any four-legged animal.

The most famous dog on wheels is

Wheely Willy, who tours all over the country with his owner, Deborah Turner. When Deborah first adopted Willy, she didn't know what to do about his paralyzed back legs. She tried different ways of helping Willy get around, like putting him on a skateboard. That didn't work too well! Then she discovered K-9 Carts, and Willy was suddenly free to run and chase and play like other dogs.

Deborah wrote a book about Willy,

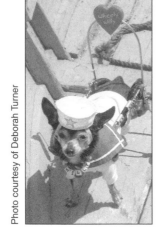

Photo courtesy of Deborah Turner

Wheely Willy

Scooter

Hockey

Photos courtesy of K-9 Carts

called *How Willy Got His Wheels*, and now he is famous. He travels with Deborah to book signings, and he is also an insured Therapy Dog, and a California Assistance Animal. He visits schools around the United States, as well as hospitals and nursing homes. He has been to movies, plays, concerts (in his tuxedo), nice restaurants, hotels, grocery stores, and is welcomed everywhere.

"People told me to put him to sleep, that he wouldn't have any kind of life, but he's had a more interesting life than any dog I know," Deborah says. "Most people noticed only what he could *not* do, and not what he might be able to do." But now Willy is out there being active and changing people's minds about what it means to use a wheelchair.

One of the many things Willy does in his full life is fly on airplanes. He was scared the first time, but he faced his fears and ended up having a grand adventure. After that, Deborah wrote a second book called *How Willy Got His Wings*. (To learn more about the Willy books, see Chapter 7.)

Just like lots of wheelchairs, the K-9 Cart can be modified for a particular disability or environment. A Chihuahua born without front legs was taught to use its back legs on a cart that converted to a walker. For mountain pets, wheels have been replaced with snow skis, and in Australia at least one K-9 Cart has been adapted for surf swimming. And beyond pets, the carts have gotten all kinds of animals moving — even rabbits, possums, goats and sheep! 🐾

Resources:
• K-9 Carts, 656 SE Bayshore Drive, Suite 2, Oak Harbor, WA 98277; 800-578-6960; www.k9carts.com
• Wheely Willy, P.O. Box 90993, Long Beach, CA 90809-0993; www. wheelywilly.com

Nicki and friends

Would you like to see a color MAGAZINE called

Kids on Wheels?

Visit us on the Web at
www.kidsonwheels.us
and let us know what you think!

Making Art

Everybody needs to express themselves. Some kids do it by talking, and some kids choose a "creative outlet" — an artistic way to express feelings and thoughts. Luckily people have found ways to adapt all the arts so that it's possible for people with disabilities to dance, act in plays, create music, make photographs and paint. There are even kids who paint *with* their wheelchairs!

Painting

Allison Cameron Gray is an artist: Her vision comes from inside, and she has to get it out. "It's about what I see and feel — not what the teacher wants," says Allison, 15. Why not just say it in words? "Color! The excitement of color and life is more vibrant when expressed in art," she says.

Because of her cerebral palsy, Allison has to be especially creative in her techniques. "I had a hard time visually and physically looking down at the desk," says Allison, who lives in Van Nuys, California. Her teacher came up with the idea of a large, heavy, slanted board that Allison's grandfather then made.

"Initially, I couldn't hold a paintbrush, so the teacher tried nail cleaner brushes with grips, potato brushes, any type of brushes with grips. My mom bought them and the teacher cut the

Allison says, "I love the freedom art gives me."

brushes so I could paint."

For mixing paint, Allison uses a baby bowl with suction cups on the bottom so she doesn't spill. When working with dry colors, she uses metal chalk holders so she doesn't snap the pastels when she grips them.

"Most importantly, the teacher would not allow my aide to do any of the work. I was on my own, no matter how the project turned out," Allison says. "I took advanced art the third year of middle school and actually got the award for most improved and best art student."

Then came high school. Although Allison showed up for class with all her adaptive equipment, her new teacher was not as open-minded as her former teacher, Ms. Michel. "The new art teacher would not talk to me, but to my aide," Allison says. "Anything I attempted, she had my aide do over. She kept on saying that the class needed 'fine motor skills.' I went home crying almost every day."

Painting by Allison Cameron Gray

But Allison didn't quit making art. Her Mom arranged for her to work with Ms. Michel after school.

Allison is disappointed about the discrimination at her new school, but the most important thing to her is that she gets to continue with her art. "I hate using the computer all day for schoolwork," she says. "With art, I don't have to have things lined up in format. I love the freedom art gives me."

To see a video about Allison and her work, go to www.lausd.k12.ca.us/ Millikan_MS/departments/art_ index.html and click on "Allison Gray's Artwork Video."

Cool Organizations

VSA Arts is one of the organizations that provides chances for people with disabilities from all over the world to express themselves through art. Especially kids! Every year VSA honors four young people with disabilities who sing or play a musical instrument with the Young Soloist Award. Those four get a free trip to Washington, D.C., to perform at the John F. Kennedy Center for the Performing Arts. There's also the Playwright Discovery Award. Students with disabilities in middle school and high school write plays about being disabled. Two of them get to go to Washington D.C. to see their plays performed at the Kennedy Center.

There are many other programs carried out by local VSA chapters. There are art exhibits, dance classes and a whole lot more. VSA has chapters in 39 states and 67 countries

VSA Arts was started in 1974 by Jean Kennedy Smith. She's the sister of John F. Kennedy, former President of the United States. At the time, VSA stood for "Very Special Arts." But now it stands for "Vision, Strength and Artistic Expression."

In 1999, when VSA turned 25 years old, they put out a book called *The Journey to Here.* It's full of stories about artists with disabilities. Some of them are kids in wheelchairs, like Stephanie Birmingham of Wisconsin. She won a VSA award for painting and she also writes poetry and dances. Stephanie says, "I tell the kids at school that I'm no different than them, and to treat me the way they treat everyone else. ... Don't look at me from the outside physically. Look at me for who I am and the being inside."

• VSA arts, 1300 Connecticut Avenue, Suite 700, Washington, D.C. 20036; 202-628-2800; 800-933-8721; 202/737-0645 (TDD); info@vsarts.org; www.vsarts.org

Painting by Melina Fatsiou-Cowan

'You Do What You Want'

Mary Kate Callahan could be called a "Renaissance girl." The Renaissance was a period of history right after the Dark Ages in which art, literature and culture thrived. To say someone is a Renaissance person means he or she is accomplished at many different things.

That describes Mary Kate to a T. At just 8 years old, she is a painter, a photographer, an actress, a singer and an athlete.

Mary Kate lives in a suburb of Chicago with her parents and her two older brothers, Jack, 12, and Kevin, 10, in a house designed for her access. When Mary Kate was 5-1/2 months old, she got a virus that entered her spinal cord and damaged it so that she has almost no use of her lower body.

Mary Kate mostly uses a manual wheelchair for mobility and to explore the world — even while she creates new worlds through her art.

She was in preschool when she discovered painting pictures. Her first painting of dragonflies was her favorite and is on display at a spinal cord research center in Miami, Florida. Right away, Mary Kate was hooked.

"It's fun because you do what you really want," she says. She prefers painting gardens and landscapes, but sometimes she has no idea what to paint. "I don't have to paint a certain thing," Mary Kate says. "If I don't know what to paint I just start painting and then it turns into something."

Some people focus all their creativity on one thing. Not Mary Kate. She also likes to take photographs and perform in front of lots of people, doing theater and singing in the choir. Last Christmas, she was part of a school play where the actors had to make up their own lines rather than memorizing a script. "It's just really fun," Mary Kate says, "to be in front all of all these people singing."

When she grows up, Mary Kate would like to be a teacher of young kids, maybe kindergarten or older. And she would pass on to them advice in the form of two quotes that mean a lot to her: "Never, never give up," and "It's perfectly perfect not to be perfect.'

—*By Mariel Garza*

"My advice is to always have an imagination because it helps when you have a disability."

— Zak Schaber, age 11. Zak has muscular dystrophy and likes to draw.

Associations

• The Association of Mouth and Foot Painting Artists exhibits and sells incredible paintings by mouth and foot painters, some of whom have received scholarships from the organization. The Web site (www.amfpa.com) also provides instructions on how to paint with your mouth.

• The Muscular Dystrophy Association has lots of paintings by disabled artists on its Web site (www.mdausa.org/commprog/art), where you can also read about the organization's art workshops for kids.

Painting by Shawna Borman/courtesy MDA

Is It Art?

Sometimes when 6-year-old Katie Hintz Kopf pushes her purple wheelchair, bubbles fly all over the place. "Sometimes the bubbles hit me in the nose," she says with a laugh.

Katie lives in a house on an island in

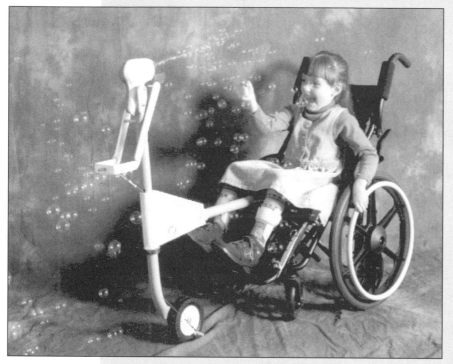

Lake Superior in Wisconsin. She makes bubbles when Dwayne Szot, an artist who lives close to her, attaches a bubble machine he invented to her chair.

The machine has three wands like the ones you find in bottles of bubbles. When she pushes her chair, it makes the sticks go up and down and they dip into a tray of bubble mix. A fan goes round and round and that's what blows the bubbles. "It kind of feels like I'm dancing," Katie says, as hundreds of bubbles float around her.

Suzy Veik of Omaha, Nebraska, is 7 years old and she has a purple wheelchair too. She made bubbles too one day when Dwayne brought the bubble maker to a

school near where she lives. That was a fun day. She also came home with paint all over her wheelchair that day. "It's still got paint on it," she says.

It's pink paint. Suzy also joined a bunch of other kids in painting a mural. There was a big piece of paper spread out on the floor and each kid got to paint a little part of it. There was a big brush with pink paint strapped to Suzy's front wheel, and when it was Suzy's turn to paint she rolled around and around on the piece of paper. That's how she got it all over her wheelchair. She says what she painted that day was partly a picture of her mom and partly a picture of her house.

Dwayne says when Katie and Suzy are making bubbles, they're making sculpture. Dwayne likes to help kids in wheelchairs figure out ways to use their wheelchairs to make art. Years ago, when he was in art school, he invented a painting wheelchair. He hooked up a power wheelchair with brushes so someone could paint just by driving it.

Today Dwayne runs a company called Zot Artz/Arts for All. He travels around helping kids make murals together. He makes and sells brushes that strap on to wheelchairs and chalk holders too. You can stick big pieces of chalk in the chalk holder and drive around and draw on the sidewalk.

• Zot Artz Arts for All, 10 S. 5th St., P.O. Box 767, Bayfield, WI 54814; 877-851-2103; www.zotartz.com/

Photography

Photography is a fun art form that just about anyone can do.

Mary Kate Callahan, who is 8, likes to takes photographs. Her first models were two of her rag dolls, one that uses a manual wheelchair like Mary Kate. "I would set them up like they're at a tea party," she says. Mary Kate also develops the pictures in a darkroom, which is a complicated process. "You dip [the prints] in different chemicals, so I have all these goggles and masks because it really smells," she laughs.

Lots of people these days like to use digital cameras instead of film cameras. Digital cameras allow you to download your pictures onto a computer, but if you want good prints, you have to use a special computer printer instead of making them in the darkroom.

People have come up with all kinds of ways for wheelchair users who can't even move their arms to still take pictures.

People who use wheelchairs have taken over a thousand pictures as part of the Picture This Photography Project in Massachusetts. Their pictures show what life looks like from a wheelchair. The first thing they did was work with a professional photographer to figure out how they could use the cameras.

One man could only move his head. He drove his power wheelchair by pushing the switch with his tongue. So he had a camera mounted to his wheelchair right in front of his face. He lined pictures up by moving his chair around and then he pushed the button on the camera with his chin or tongue.

To learn more about a mount that can attach a camera to your wheelchair, see the Access to Recreation catalog.

• Access to Recreation, 8 Sandra Court, Newbury Park, CA 91320; 800-634-4351; www.accesstr.com

• Picture This Photography Project (Web site only): www.viewinders.org

Music

Everybody likes to play the drums. Drumming is a lot of fun and it's easy to get started. All you need is something to beat on. You don't even need a stick. You can just use your hands if you want to.

Drums belong to the group of musical instruments called percussions. They are instruments you beat or shake to

Photo by Marina Parker

make a sound, like bells, cymbals and tambourines.

There are a bunch of different kinds of drums. The Disabled Drummers Association is a group that helps kids and adults with disabilities figure out what drum they want to play and how to play it.

Sometimes it's easy to figure out. Maybe if you can't hold a drumstick very well you can just strap the stick to your hand. And then you can bang away all day!

But sometimes it takes more than just a strap. So some of the companies that make drums also make things that make it easier for kids in wheelchairs to play them. Some of these things are simple and don't cost much money. Some are bigger and more expensive.

the arts

Remo is a company that makes lots of different drums for kids. One of them is the paddle drum, which is shaped like a giant lollipop. You beat it with a small mallet. They also make a clamp that can attach a paddle drum to the front of a wheelchair. If you use the clamp, you can play the paddle drum using just one hand.

Roland is a company that makes electric musical instruments. They make drum machines. The drum machines that are easy for kids in wheelchairs to play are the SPD machines. They don't take up much room. You can put them right on top of the table. They have big rubber pads on top that are easy to hit. You can record hundreds of drum sounds and other sounds into the machine, and then all you do is hit the pads with your hands or sticks to play the sounds.

There are so many different drums and so many way to play them that every kid can do it. You can be as simple or as fancy as you want to be!

• Disabled Drummers Association, 18901 NW 19 Ave., Miami, FL 33056; 305-621-9022; DDAFathertime@aol.com; www.DisabledDrummers.org

• Roland Corporation, 5100 S. Eastern Ave., Los Angeles, CA 90040-2938; 323-890-3700; www.roland.com

• Remo Inc., 28101 Industry Drive, Valencia, CA 91355; 661-294-5600; www.remo.com

Adapting Instruments

Some instruments can be played by a computer, or their sound can be copied by a computer. There are software packages and sets of switches that make it possible for kids with high levels of disability to play keyboards. For more information, check out this Web site: www.drakeonline.org.

Other adaptive techniques include building a stand to hold an instrument. That solution worked for Jessi Tomko of Whitehall, Pennsylvania. When she was in fourth grade she decided she wanted to play the flute. But she had trouble holding the flute up to play it because her arms and upper body are not strong.

"At first I just put a pillow on my wheelchair armrest," she says. She hoped that would give her better balance, but it didn't work too well. But then her music teacher made her a flute holder shaped like the letter U. Jessi clamped it to a music stand. She rested the long end of the flute on the U to hold it up, and she was able to play! Jessi got to be so good that she played flute in her middle school band.

One Canadian boy wanted to play the trumpet, but he couldn't use his hands much. An inventor came up with a stand that holds the instrument *and* a set of electric switches the boy could use to play the trumpet from his armrest.

Another invention is an adapted guitar pick for kids whose hands are weak. Most of these kinds of products are custom-made, so you probably need help from someone who likes to build things. To see the trumpet holder and guitar pick, go to www.workshopsolutions.com. You can see what the inventors did and even contact them with questions.

• Vancouver Adapted Music Society, Box 27, Suite A-304, 770 Pacific Blvd. South, Plaza of Nations, Vancouver, British Columbia, Canada V6B 5E7; 604-688-6464; vams@disabilityfoundation.org; www.reachdisability.org/vams/

Dance

"I dance all the time!" says 10-year-old Danielle Fellguth of San Bruno, California. Danielle has cerebral palsy and she loves to dance either standing on her feet or sitting in her wheelchair.

Patrick Hughes: Sharing His Gift

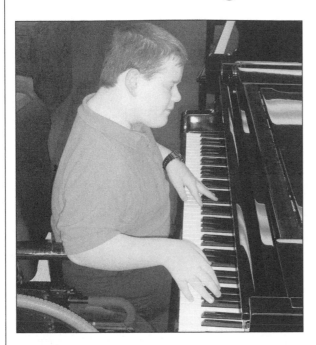

role model

When Patrick Hughes was a baby he couldn't stop crying. "Dad just couldn't figure out why," Patrick says. "And so he put me in my little playpen and put me on top of the piano and he'd play a song. I'd get quiet."

Patrick started playing piano when he was 9 months old, sitting in his high chair. And since then his life has been "music, music and more music."

He's 15 now and he plays classical music concerts on the piano. He also plays trumpet. But his favorite kinds of music are gospel and country. One of the most fun and exciting things he ever did was sing along with country music singer Pam Tillis on stage at the Grand Old Opry.

Patrick has used a wheelchair all his life because he was born with a condition where his arms and legs won't straighten out all the way. He's also been blind all his life because he was born without any eyes. "I'll tell you the good thing about being blind," he says. "I encourage people to look on the inside."

Since he can't read music on paper, he has to play everything from memory. "My piano teacher records the songs she wants me to learn," he says. "And I usually just follow along until I get it."

Patrick lives in Louisville, Kentucky, with his parents and two younger brothers. But when he was 11, he took a trip to New York to play piano on the Maury Povich television show. Visiting New York was excellent, Patrick says, not only because he got to be on television but also because he and his mom and dad got free tickets to see *Beauty and the Beast* on Broadway. But the biggest reason he loved New York was "because I love sound effects, and I heard plenty there," he says.

That's why Patrick also calls himself "a big game show watcher." He likes shows like *The Price is Right* and *Wheel of Fortune* because they have a lot of sound effects.

When Patrick grows up, he wants to be a country music singer more than anything else. But because he speaks Spanish very well, he says he also would enjoy being an interpreter. And if that doesn't work out, he wouldn't mind being a comedian or a food critic. "But I don't know if I could write a bad food review. Just about everything I put in my mouth I say, 'Mmm, that's good!'"

Meanwhile, making music for others is the life for Patrick. "I love to meet people. I always love the crowd. That's one of the reasons I like to perform so much. I like to share my gift."

Patrick sings with Lane Brody on Nashville's Riverfront Stages in June 2002.

She dances with her friends or alone listening to her CDs.

That's why in 2003 she signed up to take dancing lessons after school as part of Dance Access/KIDS! in Oakland, California. She gets to dance with other kids in wheelchairs, kids with other disabilities, and kids with no disabilities at all. In the spring of 2003 they all danced together in a live performance.

Dance Access/KIDS! is a class offered by Axis Dance Company, a ballet troupe where adults in manual and power wheelchairs dance with people who can walk. It's called "mixed abilities" dancing. When Danielle went to a performance and saw them all whirling around together, she said to herself, "Whoa! That's cool! I wanna do that!"

Danielle is such a good dancer that she's in a class for teenagers. In the spring of 2003 they did a live performance of their own. When Danielle grows up, she hopes to dance with the regular Axis troupe. In Cleveland, Ohio, there's another mixed abilities dance company called Dancing Wheels. It began as part of the Cleveland Ballet but

it's now a dance company on its own. And it's still going strong. Dancing Wheels has performed all over the world. Like Axis Dance, they also perform in classrooms and at school assemblies so kids can learn about and try wheelchair dancing.

Dancing Wheels offers classes for kids and teens in wheelchair dancing, modern dance and ballet. They even have classes called "Mommy and Me," where mothers dance with their babies as young as 1 year old.

Dancing Wheels also sells a book called *Dancing Wheels*. It tells the story of Jenny Sikora, who was wheelchair dancing when she was 11 years old.

DanceAbility is a group in Eugene, Oregon, that has helped set up mixed abilities dance companies around the world. It was started in 1979 by a dancer named Alito Alessi. Alito doesn't use a wheelchair but his mother and sister did. DanceAbility offers classes for all kids in "creative movement" as Alito calls. Alito says he is ready to come to any town to teach groups of kids or adults how to do mixed abilities dance.

• Axis Dance, 1428 Alice Street, Suite 201, Oakland, CA 94612; 510-625-0110; info@axisdance.org; axisdance.org.

• DanceAbility, Joint Forces Dance Co., P.O. Box 3686, Eugene, OR 97403; 541-342-3273; alito22@yahoo.com; www.streamcommunication. com/danceability

• Dancing Wheels, Professional Flair, 3615 Euclid Ave., 3rd Floor, Cleveland, OH 44115; 216-432-0306; proflair1@ aol.com; www.gggreg.com/ dancingwheels.htm

Stephen didn't realize just how big a ham he was until he started performing in live theater!

Theater

One day in 1997, Stephen Hiatt-Leonard of Evanston, Illinois, went to a show put on by the world famous Joffrey Ballet. He was excited to see that people who used wheelchairs like him were dancing in the ballet too.

So Stephen decided to try out for a part in the Joffrey's Christmas ballet "The Nutcracker." Lots of kids get to be in The Nutcracker every year. "Why not me?" Stephen thought.

And Stephen got the part! And every year for the next five years he played the part of one of the party guests in The Nutcracker. He didn't have any lines but he did get to pretend like he was playing the horn. Stephen is 15 now and today he performs in a show called Six Stories Up.

Every year, Six Stories Up gets a group of kids in Chicago, some with disabilities like Stephen, together with a group of adults and they write and perform stories on stage. Six Stories Up was created by an actress named Tekki Lomnicki. She's a woman who is only 41 inches tall and walks with crutches.

Stephen wrote a story for Six Stories Up about two brothers. Stephen played the part of the brother in a wheelchair. The other brother got mad because their mother treated him differently. She was harder on him. She would make him do chores Stephen didn't have to do. And Stephen was mad because he thought Mom let the other brother do more fun things. In the end, Mom decided to let Stephen grow up and not treat him differently from his brother.

Stephen loves performing and he wants to do it for a long time. But he only wants to do it for fun. "I do it because I get to meet a lot of wonderful people, " he says.

Another place where kids with and without disabilities perform together is Imagination Stage in Bethesda, Maryland. Imagination Stage puts on plays written for young people. But they also offer a lot of different classes where kids learn to sing, dance and act. And if they get to be good enough they might even get to be in one of the plays starring kids put on by Imagination Stage every year. The AccessAbility Theatre Program is designed especially to help kids with disabilities learn how to perform.

• Imagination Stage (Main Office/Box Office); 4908 Auburn Ave., Bethesda, MD 20814; 301-961-6060 301/718-8813 (TTY); info@imagination stage.org; www.imaginationstage.org

• Six Stories Up, Tellin Tales Theater, 360 East Randolph St., Suite 1006, Chicago, IL 60601; 312-409-1025; info@ tellintales.org; www.tellintales.org

MIKE ERVIN is a freelance writer in Chicago. He has muscular dystrophy and uses a power chair.

kids on screen

By Jeff Shannon

The Power of Media Images

In some ways, movies and TV are like windows to the world. They can show reality (like a documentary film) or fantasy (like "The Lord of the Rings"). They make it all seem equally believable, and they can help us to understand people and places we've never seen. For kids who use wheelchairs, movies and TV often show the attitudes of the society they live in.

In the old days, stories like "A Christmas Carol" showed kids with disabilities as weak. "Tiny Tim" was like this, and society felt sorry for him and treated him as helpless. Many of the earliest movies depicted adults with disabilities as evil villains, driven to crime and madness by their physical differences.

Beginning in the 1950s, TV fund-raising telethons (like the Jerry Lewis telethons to support a cure for muscular dystrophy) made kids in wheelchairs seem like objects of pity. Viewers were encouraged to think of them as "pathetic" kids who can't do the things that "normal" kids do.

Fortunately, TV and movies are always changing to reflect new and (hopefully) more accepting attitudes about people who use wheelchairs. As society "grows up" and learns more about disabilities, TV and movies are becoming more realistic.

Even though some of the "pity" stereotypes still exist, more and more

Realistic images show that wheelchair users have the same hopes and dreams as everyone.

"Miracle in Lane 2" is based on the real-life story of 12-year-old Justin Yoder, a wheelchair user who wants to win a sports trophy.

movies and TV shows are showing wheelchair users as real, normal people who have the same goals, dreams and desires as everyone else. Shows like "Pelswick" and "Malcolm in the Middle" — and even "grown-up" cartoons like "South Park" — show disabled people as they really are — good, bad, happy, sad. In other words, they're not defined or limited by their disability. And they have more in common with the nondisabled people around them. As this progress continues, movies and TV — and society in general — will be more comfortable with people in wheelchairs. This helps everyone to see people with disabilities for who they really are, and not as people to feel sorry for.

On the Tube

Pelswick

"Pelswick" was a smart, funny cartoon that made an important breakthrough in how it showed kids with disabilities. (It was on TV from October 2000 to November 2002.) The title character of this half-hour series was Pelswick Eggert, a regular 13-year-old kid who just happened to use a wheelchair. (Or, as Pelswick liked to say, "I'm permanently seated!"). Apart from his disability, Pelswick was just another normal 8th-grader who enjoyed all the

things that other kids enjoy. And like a lot of kids he had a knack for getting into trouble! For one thing, he had to put up with the local bully, Boyd Scullarzo, who was always teasing and insulting Pelswick. Boyd was kind of a dummy, though, and Pelswick had no problem fighting back, because he was a lot smarter than Boyd and his dimwitted pals, Nick and Joe.

Pelswick also had some good friends of his own, including his best friends, Ace and Goon. He also had a big crush on Julie, a cute classmate who was always there to cheer Pelswick up when he needed support. At home, Pelswick got more support from his crazy grandmother, Gram-Gram. His father was funny because he was always trying to be "politically correct" so he wouldn't offend anyone. Pelswick also had a guardian angel named Mister Jimmy, who would appear at any time (only Pelswick could see him). But Mr. Jimmy's wacky advice wasn't much help, so Pelswick did his best to avoid him!

"Pelswick" was produced in Canada and created by the American cartoonist, John Callahan, who uses a wheelchair. "For Pelswick, being in a wheelchair is no big deal," Callahan once said. "I just wanted him to be seen as a normal kid, doing all the things that other kids do." To achieve that goal, Callahan worked closely with the writers of the show. He made sure Pelswick always presented a positive image of a kid in a wheelchair — a kid who would have ups ands downs and fun adventures, just like his friends. Pelswick also reflected a lot of the humor that Callahan expressed in his own cartoons: sarcastic, witty, and always prone to mischief!

"Pelswick" lasted for a total of 26 episodes before it was canceled in late 2002. The show had a lot of loyal viewers, and it will remain an important mile-stone in the positive portrayal of kids with disabilities.

Malcolm in the Middle

The popular TV sitcom "Malcolm in the Middle" premiered on the Fox network in the fall of 2000. From its very first episode it featured the popular character Stevie, a kid in a wheelchair. Played by young actor Craig Lamar Traylor, Stevie is in the "gifted students" class for smart kids. That's where he first met Malcolm (played by Frankie

Muniz), and the two boys became good friends despite the fact that Malcolm was reluctant at first.

Stevie's smart, resourceful, and funny, but he's also got asthma, which makes him short of breath. He's always taking deep breaths and talks very slowly. That doesn't seem to bother Stevie, so

The more wheelers we see on TV, the more comfortable the world becomes with us.

it doesn't bother Malcolm, either. And because Stevie's highly intelligent, he always seems to know how to solve the many problems that Malcolm gets into.

Stevie in "Malcolm in the Middle" was groundbreaking because Stevie is shown to be "just one of the guys," and he gets to go with Malcolm and other kids on a lot of funny misadventures. Being in a wheelchair and having asthma never stops Stevie from having fun. One time he even got caught in an underground storm drain with Malcolm!

Stevie also has some problems, just like other kids: His parents tend to be overprotective (which happens to a lot of kids in wheelchairs). Mostly, though, Stevie's just a kid like any other kid — he's got strengths and weaknesses. He's not always right, he can make fun of himself, and he knows he's not perfect.

"Malcolm in the Middle" is a big step forward in the way TV shows people with disabilities. By showing Stevie as someone who has a solid group of friends, this popular and funny TV series proves that the social acceptance of disability is always getting better.

Other TV

"Pelswick" and "Malcolm in the Middle" are just two examples of a positive trend: More and more characters in wheelchairs are appearing in films and TV. What's even better is that these characters are often shown to be active participants in their society. In other words, their disability isn't the main focus of who they are. They're not

defined by their friends and family simply in terms of being disabled. They're just accepted for who they are.

These characters allow people to understand what it's like to use a wheelchair. It helps them realize that people who use wheelchairs are a lot like them.

In the popular TV series "Ed," which ended this year, Daryl Mitchell played Eli, a wheelchair user who is the manager of the bowling alley. Mitchell was a successful rapper and actor before he was paralyzed in a motorcycle accident in 2001. His regular role on "Ed" makes him one of the most prominent disabled actors in the world. Just like his character on TV, Mitchell didn't get any special treatment from the cast and crew of "Ed"

— they helped him when he needed it, but otherwise they accepted him just as he is, wheelchair and all.

Wheelchair-using characters were also featured in the recent (but now canceled) TV series "Dark Angel" (now available on DVD) and "Birds of Prey." In both shows, the disabled characters were played by nondisabled actors, and they played a familiar stereotype: the wheelchair-user who relies heavily on technology for their daily activities. But this time the image was positive: With lots of computers and high-tech equipment, these wheelchair users were highly skilled and intelligent. They gained freedom and independence from technology, and that happens in real life, too.

In the TV series "Joan of Arcadia," the lead character is a teenager whose 19-year-old brother, Kevin, was injured in a car accident. Now he's a paraplegic who uses a wheelchair. As the series began, Kevin was still angry and bitter about being disabled. He wouldn't leave the house, go to school, or get a job.

But he gradually learned to accept his disability, and he slowly recovered — not physically but emotionally. He took an interest in life again, learning and adapting to his disability so he could become a productive member of society. As this new TV series went forward, it promised a more honest, accurate, and positive depiction of what it's like to be a young person in a wheelchair. It also showed that being disabled is not always easy. In fact, sometimes it's really, really hard!

Although it's still hard for many actors in wheelchairs to find work in films and TV, things are improving. As more wheelchair users appear in TV and movies, people in wheelchairs will find more comfort and acceptance in the world around them.

In the Movies

Unfortunately, there haven't been many movies that show kids in wheelchairs. The main reason is, movies cost a lot to make, and they have to attract a very large audience in order to make a profit. That's why the big movie studios make expensive "blockbuster" movies like "Spider-Man" and "The Lord of the Rings."

As popular as these movies might be, they don't leave much room for smaller movies about people who use wheelchairs. Disability is not a "glamorous" subject, so it's considered "risky" by the studios that make movies. As a result, the movies that show people who use wheelchairs are likely to be TV movies or the kind of smaller movies made by independent filmmakers. Those movies don't cost as much money to make, so they can tell the kinds of stories that might not appeal to the mass audience for big-budget "blockbuster" movies.

When movies show someone who uses a wheelchair, they're mostly young adults, grown-ups and older people. Kids in wheelchairs are not seen in movies very often at all. There are some exceptions, though, and here are a few examples:

Miracle in Lane 2

This was a TV movie that was originally shown on the Disney channel in the year 2000, and it's now available on video. This movie is based on the real-life story of Justin Yoder, a young boy who uses a wheelchair because of spina bifida. Frankie Muniz (from TV's "Malcolm in the

Middle") plays Justin, who is 12 years old and badly wants to win a sports trophy. He decides to race a wooden car in the local "Soap Box Derby." In some ways this story shows a familiar stereotype, since Justin is shown as an "inspirational" kid who learns to accept and overcome his disability. But overall, this is a pretty good movie that shows some of the difficulties of being a kid in a wheelchair.

Mac and Me

This 1988 movie is one of the few (maybe the only) films to star a child actor who uses a wheelchair in real life. Jade Calegory, who has spina bifida, plays Eric, a boy who moves with his mother and older brother to California. While they're on their way, a friendly young alien (Mac) hitches a ride in their van and becomes a part of Eric's life. This movie will remind you of "E.T." and will probably make you hungry for a Big Mac and a Coke because of how often they show those products. But on the up-side, it shows a kid in a wheelchair who has a lot more going on in his life than his disability. Unfortunately, the way the story is written, you care more about the alien than Eric, but there are some cool scenes where Eric uses his wheelchair to outwit the bad guys chasing him and Mac.

Gaby: A True Story

First released in 1987 and now available on video, this is one of the best movies ever made about a young person in a wheelchair. It tells the true story of Gaby Brimmer, a girl who is almost completely paralyzed by cerebral palsy. This is a very serious movie because it deals very honestly with all of the hard-

ships of Gaby's disability, but it also shows how much she is able to accomplish in her life because she didn't give up or feel sorry for herself. The role of parents and teachers is also important: They support Gaby without feeling sorry for her, and they help her to achieve her goals.

Jade Calegory, who has spina bifida, is one of the few real wheelchair users to star in a movie.

Simon Birch

Released in 1998, "Simon Birch" is one of those movies that will probably make you cry. In this case that's a good thing! The movie was inspired by a novel called *A Prayer For Owen Meaney*, written by John Irving, and it's about two boys who see themselves as misfits. In other words, they don't really fit in at home or at school, so they find a fun and adventurous friendship with each other. One of them is Joe (played by young actor Joseph Mazello, from the movie "Jurassic Park"), and he never knew his

father. His friend Simon Birch (played by Ian Michael Smith) is a dwarf (sometimes called a "little person") and although he doesn't use a wheelchair, he feels "different" from other kids. This is a movie about accepting your own differences and, in some ways, turning them into strengths. After all, what makes you different is also what makes you ...YOU!

Finding Nemo

You've probably already seen this box-office hit from 2003, about a little fish named Nemo whose father is overprotective because Nemo has a "special" fin on his right side that's a lot smaller than the one on his left side — kind of like having a disabled arm or a leg. When Nemo is caught by a human and put in a fish tank, he learns to overcome his disability with courage and hard work, and he proves that he can swim just like all the other fish. This is also a good movie for parents, because it teaches them that being too careful or overprotective can have a negative effect on

kids, who grow and learn by doing new and different things that might seem scary at first. "Finding Nemo" is about gaining confidence in yourself despite your fears and disability, so you can feel better about exploring the big, mysterious world around you!

Just the Way You Are

"Just the Way You Are" is a 1984 movie about a young woman who feels embarrassed because she has a disabled leg. She hasn't accepted her disability, so she tries to hide it from other people. This only causes further trouble and confusion when she finally has to reveal her disabled leg, so she learns that she should just accept her disability and let it be a part of who she is. If you're a kid in a wheelchair you might think that a disabled leg is no big deal, but this movie is still worthwhile in showing how important it is to accept your disability and not feel bad about it.

The Horse Whisperer

"The Horse Whisperer" is about a girl who has an accident that results in the partial amputation of one of her legs. She has a horse that was disabled in the same accident, and with the help of a very special horse trainer, the horse is healed and the girl learns to accept her disability. This is a very good movie that teaches basically the same lesson as "Just the Way You Are" — that having a disability, no matter how big or small, is not something to be ashamed of. (This movie is rated PG-13 because of the accident scene, which some kids may find upsetting.)

There are two other movies — "Dark Horse," (1992) and "Second Chances" (a 1998 TV movie) — that are a lot like "The Horse Whisperer." You might be able to find them in larger video stores or by shopping on the Internet.

Allison Cameron Gray: 'Not a Passing Fancy'

Allison Cameron Gray caught the "acting bug" at a very early age, and she'd be the first to remind you, "it's not a passing fancy." Allison was born with cerebral palsy, and she needed several years of speech therapy (in addition to physical and occupational therapy) to overcome the challenges of her disability. Although she can use a walker for short distances, she uses a wheelchair most of the time.

Allison's parents are divorced, so the 15-year-old Californian divides her time living with her mom in Van Nuys, and her dad in Sherman Oaks (both are suburbs of Los Angeles).

At first, Allison's mother was against the idea of acting, because she feared Allison would get discouraged by the rejection that all actors must go through. When Allison was 9, her mom finally allowed her to attend an acting class. "I've been hooked ever since," says Allison, who has appeared as "background talent" on the Disney Channel TV series "That's So Raven" and the Fox high-school drama "Boston Public." She also made a guest appearance on the TV series "Family Law," in addition to appearing in smaller industrial films while she continues to study acting.

"I enjoy transforming myself into different people," says Allison, who's also an honor student in school. "Acting is like art, only the actor is the canvas." Still, Allison is aware that people with disabilities are often stereotyped as "pitiful," and she works hard to promote a more positive image for those who use wheelchairs. "I do think I have to be a positive role model," she says, "because if I continue to play into the stereotypes, attitudes will not change."

Allison is aware that some people treat her differently because she uses a wheelchair, and she thinks that people with disabilities will be accepted if TV and movies portray them with no special treatment, just like everyone else. "I'm not interested in playing the helpless, dependent person who brings out pity in the viewer," she says. "People with different abilities need to be shown as whole people — as a part of the community. It's slowly changing, but not fast enough for me."

Allison has a lot of goals, and there's one kind of role she'd really enjoy: "I'd really like to play a villain," she says. "I think it would show the audience that people with different abilities are not always sweet and innocent, as well as give me an opportunity to show my acting skills."

Allison has good advice for wheelchair-using kids who want to break into show business: "Be prepared for rejection, and take most jobs if they don't conflict with your values. Take the opportunity to watch and learn, and use your non-working time to take classes, appear in local plays, speak up in class — anything that allows you practice your craft."

Grown-up Movies Worth Seeing
(if your parents say it's OK!)

My Left Foot

Based on the true story of Irish artist and writer Christy Brown, this is a powerful story about growing up with cerebral palsy. The title, in case you're wondering, refers to the fact that Christy can move only his left foot. He struggles to express himself and experience everything life has to offer at a time when most kids with CP were put in institutions. His family couldn't bear to do that, though, and Christy's relationship with his supportive mom is one of the best parts of the film. (This movie is rated "R" for some adult situations, so ask your parents to preview it. When they think you're old enough, make sure to rent it!)

The Elephant Man

Based on a true story, this is a great movie about a very good man who was born with a rare condition that made him physically disfigured and very different from the "normal"-looking people around him. To them he looks very ugly, and they think he's a "freak" or a "monster," and they call him "Elephant Man" because his skin and facial features are elephant-like. He becomes a social outcast in a circus "freak show," but when a nice doctor arranges to help him, he discovers that the "Elephant Man" is really kind, smart, talented, and interested in many different things. This is a sad movie in some ways, but it also shows

2004 Release: 'Saved!'

Actor Macaulay Culkin is best known for his role as the little boy left behind in "Home Alone," but lately he's been getting into a different kind of trouble. In "Saved!" he plays Roland, a smart-mouthed wheelchair user at a Christian high school.

"I liked the story and overall message," Culkin says in the film's production notes. "It's about love and faith in more ways than just about a specific religion. I thought it was wonderful and that Roland was a very charming character."

Culkin describes how Roland's character grows. At the beginning of the movie, his sister takes advantage of him "by dragging him around as if he were some kind of merit badge just to prove what a good Christian she is." But Roland isn't satisfied with that kind of life. "He's just trying to find himself, and trying to find love and friendship in his life," Culkin says. Roland grows much more independent as the film goes on.

Many of the religious and romantic themes may

be a little too old for grade-schoolers, which is why the movie is PG-13. This is another one that your parents should probably watch first to see if you're ready, but when you are, it's a fun one!

that being very different is NOT a bad thing. It's not about being disabled, but about accepting ourselves and other people for who they are.

Rear Window, The Bone Collector

These are two movie thrillers about men who are quadriplegics who use their intelligence and new technology to help them to deal with their disabilities. "Rear Window" is a 1998 remake of an older movie that was directed by Alfred Hitchcock, and it stars real-life quadriplegic Christopher Reeve as a man who thinks he's witnessed a murder ... and the killer comes after him! "The Bone Collector" (rated "R") stars Denzel Washington as a disabled forensics detective who is learning to accept his disability by using technology to help a rookie police officer (Angelina Jolie) track down a serial killer. These aren't movies about disability so much as being smart and resourceful when faced with a physical limitation.

JEFF SHANNON has been a quadriplegic since he was paralyzed in a diving accident two weeks before his 18th birthday. He quickly realized that writing would play a big role in his future. For most of his career, Jeff has been a film critic and feature writer, interviewing many different actors and filmmakers, and also writing about life with a disability. He currently lives near Seattle, Washington, and spends most of his time watching and reviewing DVDs for Amazon.com.

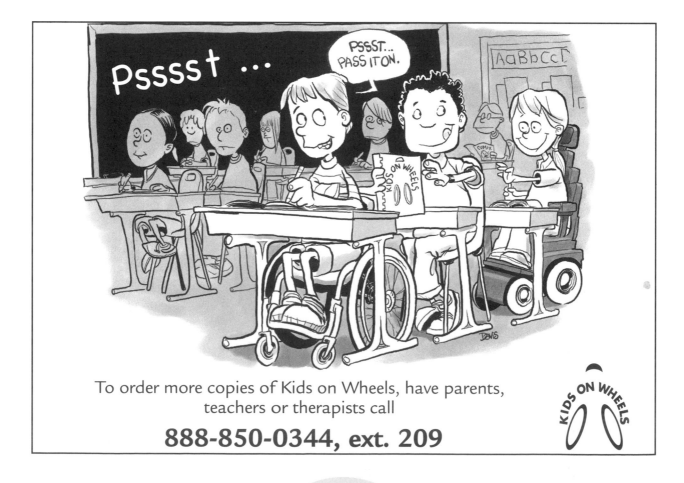

To order more copies of Kids on Wheels, have parents, teachers or therapists call

888-850-0344, ext. 209

I DON'T HAVE MUSCULAR DYSTROPHY

BUT I'M ONE OF "JERRY'S KIDS"

I have spinal muscular atrophy. It's one of the over 30 other muscle and nerve destroying diseases covered by the Muscular Dystrophy Association in addition to the muscular dystrophies themselves. That gives me and tens of thousands like me with other neuromuscular diseases the same help through MDA clinics, summer camps and support groups, and the same hope through MDA's worldwide research program.

books

By Jean Dobbs

The Story of Books

Before people wrote books, they told each other stories. It's just one of those things that we have a need to do, whether it's by talking, writing or making movies — we need to share stories.

When someone writes made-up stories, we call them *fiction*. When someone writes true stories, we call them *nonfiction*. Nonfiction also includes information that is not really a story (like most of the chapters of this book).

This chapter describes fiction and nonfiction books that include kids who use wheelchairs. For each fiction book, there is a *plot* line, which tells you basically what happens in the story. For each nonfiction book, there is a *format* line, which tells you how the information is presented.

For each book, there is a *review,* which tells you what we at *Kids on Wheels* think about it. Does it show kids who use wheelchairs in a positive way? Does it show disability in a realistic way? Does it help the reader understand something about disability? And also — is it just a good story?

If you like the way a book sounds and want to read it, you can find it in a couple of ways. First, you can try the public library. If the librarian can't find the title you're looking for, most of these books can be bought on Amazon.com (ask your parents to help you order them).

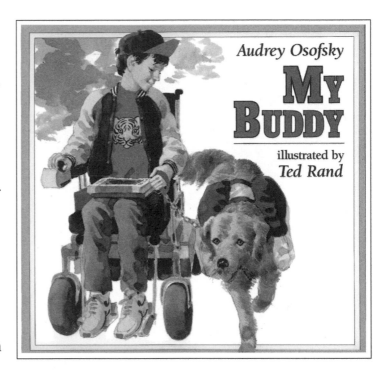

Audrey Osofsky
My Buddy
illustrated by **Ted Rand**

Picture Books: Ages 4-8

Fiction

My Buddy
By Audrey Osofsky
1992
Plot: A boy with muscular dystrophy increases his independence with a service dog.
Review: This is a realistic story about training, working with and loving a ser-

vice dog. You could use it to learn more about service dogs or show it to other kids if you get a service dog. The pictures are good watercolors, but there are some that don't make sense, like the boy taking a shower in a manual wheelchair instead of a shower chair.

Little Tree
By Joyce C. Mills
1992

Plot: A tree loses a limb in a storm and must adjust to disability.

Review: This is a beautiful book about emotional healing when physical recovery is not possible. It deals well with facing fears and that "why me?" feeling. Little Tree is a lovable character who learns that she still has much to offer the world.

Nick Joins In
By Joe Lasker
1980

Plot: Nick is afraid to join a full-inclusion class, but then starts to enjoy school. He uses his intelligence to help the other kids out of a jam.

Review: This book is a bit *dated* — which means it doesn't show things as they are today. For example, Nick's wheelchair looks very old-fashioned. The story is a little nicey-nice — it doesn't deal with teasing or any really difficult situations. But it

does show a kid on wheels who is smart, fun and helpful to others.

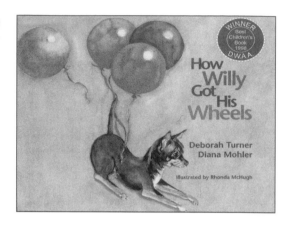

How Willy Got His Wheels
By Deborah Turner and Diana Mohler
1996

Plot: A paralyzed dog is adopted and given mobility devices that don't work. One day, he gets a wheelchair and is able to play like other dogs.

Review: Based on a true story (see page 72), this is a great tale about how a loving home and the right equipment can make a joyful life possible. Bright watercolor pictures.

How Willy Got His Wings
By Deborah Turner and Diana Mohler
2003

Plot: Willy flies on a plane for the first time, gets lost in the airport and meets his adoptive grandparents.

Review: This is another exciting story

about Wheely Willy's adventures. This one also deals with facing fears, being different and wondering if you are lovable. The pictures aren't as good as the first Willy book.

Howie Helps Himself
By Joan Fassler
1975
Plot: A boy with cerebral palsy wants to move his wheelchair by himself.

Review: The only good thing about this book is the title. Everything else is very *dated*: Howie is kind of whiny and sad and weak. He is stuck in a separate "special ed" class, and he has low goals. The book also talks down to readers — it definitely does not get the *Kids on Wheels* stamp of approval.

Rolling Along with Goldilocks and the Three Bears
By Cindy Meyers
1999
Plot: In this new twist on the familiar tale, Baby Bear uses a wheelchair and a motorized bed. Goldilocks and Baby Bear become friends.
Review: This book shows adaptive equipment pretty realistically, and there's lots of stuff about physical therapy (it was written by a physical therapist!). Overall this is a fun new look at an old story. Nice color pictures.

Sosu's Call
By Meshack Asara
1997
Plot: When a big storm threatens an African village, a paralyzed boy named Sosu saves the day.
Review: This book gives an interesting view of how disability is treated in another culture. Sosu is not included very often, but when he shows his resourcefulness during the emergency, the villagers respect him. They appreciate him so much that they get him a wheelchair and make the village accessible. The pictures are kind of rough, but this is a very good story.

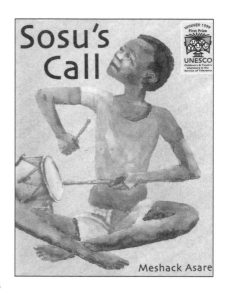

Imagine Me on a Sit-Ski
By George Moran
1995
Plot: A kid with cerebral palsy learns to ski with adaptive equipment.
Review: This is a dated book with a weak plot. It is mostly educational (about skiing) but the equipment is old. The pictures aren't very good either.

Rebecca Finds a New Way
By Connie Panzarino and Marilyn Lash
1994
Plot: Rebecca gets a spinal cord injury

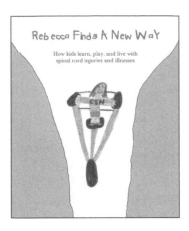

in a car crash and struggles to understand her new life with the help of her talking rabbit, Terry. **Review:** This book is a little weird because it tries to explain spinal cord injury very realistically but then again, it has a talking rabbit! The information is good, though — it deals with paralysis, bowel and bladder function, ventilators, physical therapy and more. It was published by the National Spinal Cord Injury Association.

Nonfiction

We Can Do It!
By Laura Dwight
1992
Format: Five kids with disabilities talk about their lives in their own words. There are several photos of each kid.
Review: The colorful pictures of active kids make this a fun book. Gina, who has spina bifida, paints, rides a trike, plays with her dollhouse and goes to the beach. Emiliano, who has cerebral palsy, plays with his cat, has pillow fights with his parents and pushes his walker through a sprinkler when it's hot. This is a good book for teachers to read to a first or second grade class.

It's OK to Be Different
By Todd Parr
2001
Format: Cartoons show differences between kids with the statement "It's OK to be ... "
Review: This may be a good book for little kids, but it's not very interesting because it just repeats "It's OK" about a million times. One 4-year-old says he likes to take it to school to help him explain his disability to the other kids because along with all the differences that are OK, "it's OK to have wheels."

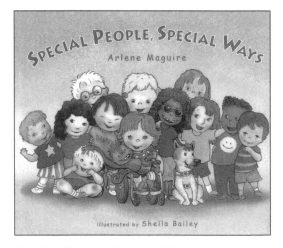

Special People, Special Ways
By Arlene Maguire
2000

Format: This is a rhyming book about how people with differences need love and understanding just like everyone else.

Review: This is a simple, "feel-good" book like *It's OK to Be Different.*

Review: This book gives good advice, like asking people if they want help instead of just helping them. This would be a good book to give to a new friend.

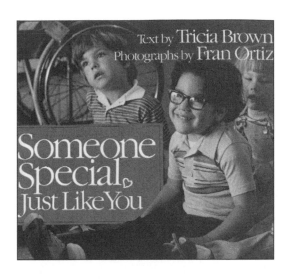

Someone Special, Just Like You
By Tricia Brown
1982

Format: Short sentences about the things all kids have in common, with photos of kids with different disabilities.
Review: Even though the pictures are more than 20 years old, they are still nice black-and-white photos of kids with disabilities enjoying life. Good for a first or second grade class.

Extraordinary Friends
By Fred Rogers
2000
Format: Advice on how to meet and make friends with a kid who has a disability. Color photos show friendships as they grow.

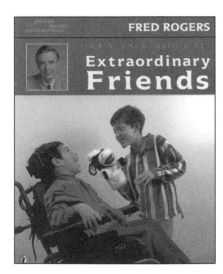

Aunt Katie's Visit
By Katie Rodriguez Banister
2003

Format: A girl tells about her aunt's visit to her class. Her aunt uses a wheelchair and talks about how she and other people with disabilities do different things.
Review: This is a good general introduction to disabilities written by a person who uses a wheelchair. You might want your teacher to read this book to your second or third grade class.

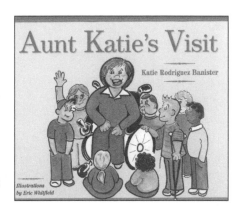

Rolling Along
By Jamee Riggio Heelan
2000

Format: This is a true story of how cerebral palsy affects a boy named Taylor. Getting a wheelchair helps him be more independent.

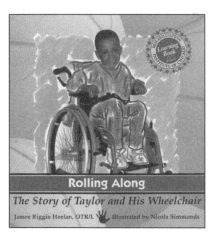

Review: This is an educational book that you might read at physical therapy or if you are about to get your first wheelchair. Otherwise, the only interesting thing is the nice relationship between Taylor and his twin brother, Tyler.

books

Taking Cerebral Palsy to School
By Mary Elizabeth Anderson
2000

Format: A boy explains what it's like to have CP.
Review: If you have CP, this is an educational book you might want your teacher to read to your class so that other kids can understand your physical and speech differences.

Chapter Books: Ages 8-12

Fiction

The Gun Lake Adventure Series
By Johnnie Tuitel and Sharon Lamson

Book 1: The Barn at Gun Lake (1998)
Book 2: Mystery Explosion! (1998)
Book 3: Blackbird Island (2000)
Book 4: Noonday Trail (2000)
Book 5: Bear Tooth Mountains (2003)

This mystery series features a young hero with cerebral palsy who uses a manual wheelchair. In the first book, Johnnie Jacobson, 11, moves from California to Michigan, where he must prove himself to the neighborhood kids. Most of them are accepting of his disability, but the Gun Lake Gang's leader, Travis, thinks Johnnie has nothing to offer the group. But Johnnie, resourceful and loyal, is a key player in discovering the truth behind the mystery at the barn, and in stopping the crooks. The authors (one of whom has CP) do a good job of integrating Johnnie's disability concerns into the story so that most of the talk about his wheelchair seems natural. This is a great start to a strong series that follows the Gun Lake Gang through numerous adventures, while painting a realistic picture of an active, independent kid on wheels. (To read part of the first book, see page 106.)

Chelsey and the Green-Haired Kid
By Carol Gorman
1987

Plot: A boy is murdered at a junior high basketball game, but most people think it was an accident. Chelsey, a 13-year-old wheelchair user, investigates the mystery and seeks the help of a new boy at school, a loner with green hair.

Review: Chelsey is a likeable, assertive girl who has adjusted well to her spinal cord injury, and she makes a strong, believable narrator. Her love-hate relationship with Jack proves that she is like any 13-year-old girl trying to understand the mystery of the opposite sex. But it is the murder mystery that propels the story, and it's not bad either. Some of the disability stuff is dated (they use the word "handicapped," and Jack pushes Chelsey's chair at times when he doesn't need to), but overall the book is a fun read.

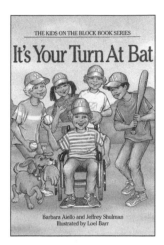

THE KIDS ON THE BLOCK BOOK SERIES

It's Your Turn At Bat

Barbara Aiello and Jeffrey Shulman
Illustrated by Loel Barr

It's Your Turn at Bat
By Barbara Aiello and Jeffrey Shulman
1988

Plot: A boy with cerebral palsy loses his baseball team's jersey money. He asks for help from a new friend who is teaching him to sew.
Review: The best part of this book is the character of Mark, an active wheelchair user who is a sports editor and team manager at his school. He's well-liked and open-minded but also has flaws like everyone else. The plot is a bit of a "stretch" (hard to believe), and the pictures are pretty old-fashioned, but this is a positive story and worth reading.

A Contest
By Sherry Neuwith Payne
1982
Plot: Mike, who has cerebral palsy, shows the kids in his class that he can play to win when he gets the chance.
Review: This is a pretty realistic story about trying to make friends. Mike goes

from "spaz" to player (arm wrestling, checkers, pool), and the book does a good job of showing his struggle for acceptance. Unfortunately, the pictures are very gray and old-looking.

Margaret's Moves
By Berniece Rabe
1987
Plot: 9-year-old Margaret schemes to buy a sports wheelchair that her family can't afford.
Review: Margaret, who has spina bifida, is clever, and her goal is worthy. But this book is kind of "stiff" — the people don't talk the way real people do, and there are lots of lectures from the adults in the story. Some of the things they say make sense, like "you are responsible for your own happiness." Some of the pictures don't make sense at all: In one, the "sports model" Margaret wants looks like an old square steel wheelchair! But Margaret is a cool kid and makes the story worth reading.

Margaret's Moves
by Berniece Rabe
illustrated by Julie Downing

Kidnapping Kevin Kowalski
By Mary Jane Auch
1990
Plot: After Kevin is in a disabling accident, his friends rescue him from his overprotective mom.
Review: Kevin isn't a wheelchair user or the hero of this story. It's told from the point of view of Kevin's best friend, Ryan, who is trying to understand how his friend has changed and to help him be more independent from his mother. This isn't the greatest book, but

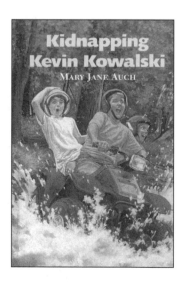

Kidnapping Kevin Kowalski
MARY JANE AUCH

if you're curious how a new disability might seem to those around you, it may give you some clues.

Nonfiction

Disabilities, Dragons and Other Magical Discoveries: A Kid's Guide to Understanding and Living with Disabilities
By Rick Enright
1998

Format: Easy-to-understand descriptions of physical disabilities and health conditions. Illustrated with lots of funny drawings.

See a section from this book on page 107.

Review: This is a great book for helping kids understand cerebral palsy, muscular dystrophy, spina bifida and spinal cord injuries. It includes info on bladder and bowel issues, as well as communication, mobility and health advice. It also has an excellent section on social life and independence. And the pictures will make you laugh while you learn. For ordering info, go to www.tvcc.on.ca/newdocs/innovations6.html.

Chapter Books: Age 10 and up

Fiction

Under the Shadow
By Anne Knowles
1983

Plot: 15-year-old Cathy helps find a

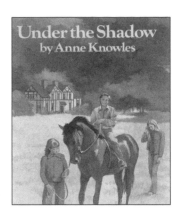

horse for her new friend, Mark, who has muscular dystrophy.
Review: Although at first glance this might sound like another story about a nondisabled person "saving" a person with a disability, it's actually a mutual friendship that brings a lot to both Mark and Cathy. Witty and brutally honest, Mark is a well-rounded character with a quick sense of humor as well as the ability to speak openly about his pain. Cathy is a smart, sensitive girl who appreciates her friend in all his complexity. It is surprising that this book is more than 20 years old — it was way ahead of its time.

Jodie's Journey
By Colin Theile
1988

Plot: 11-year-old Jodie, who competes in horse riding events, gets juvenile rheumatoid arthritis. She must give up her passion and adapt to her disability.
Review: Written by an adult with the same painful disability, this book does a good job of showing the effects of RA on a young athlete, her family and friends. Jodie endures terrible pain,

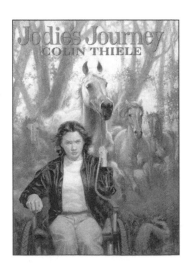

endless medical procedures, teasing at school, family fighting and the loss of her greatest passion — and still must face yet another brutal test of her resourcefulness. By the end of the book, when Jodie is 19, the message is clear: Not only can you survive disability, you can thrive as well.

Nonfiction

From Where I Sit:
Making My Way with Cerebral Palsy
By Shelly Nixon
1999

Format: Shelly tells her own life story, which makes the book an *autobiography*.

Review: Written by a smart young woman (age 21), this book starts before Shelly was born.

Shelly describes her early medical complications, her parents' fears, her diagnosis and therapy. But the heart of the book is Shelly's struggle to prove her intelligence and abilities. People think her slow speech means she is mentally disabled, and they think her quadriplegia makes her helpless. Neither is true, and Shelly proves it by winning writing awards and living an adventurous life. But Shelly also talks about her fears — like when she had to get surgeries — and her disappointments. The result is a positive book, but one that deals honestly with difficulty.

Poetry

Heartsongs (2001)
Hope Through Heartsongs (2002)
Journey Through Heartsongs (2002)
Celebrate Through Heartsongs (2002)
Loving Through Heartsongs (2003)
By Mattie J.T. Stepanek

Format: Poems and paintings.
Review: These are not books *about* disability — they are books *by* a kid with a disability. Mattie J.T. Stepanek had a rare form of muscular dystrophy (see his profile in Chapter 1). He started writing poetry when he was 3, and he published his first book at age 11. Now, poetry is not everyone's favorite thing, but these are poems that remind us to enjoy life's little pleasures and gifts. Sometimes we all need to be reminded to "smell a rainbow," or "drift like a leaf," and "listen to the song in our heart."

> Sometimes we all need to be reminded to 'smell a rainbow,' or 'drift like a leaf.'

Mystery, Adventure ... and Disability

Here is a section from The Barn at Gun Lake, *the first of five books in the Gun Lake Adventure Series (described on page 102). A sixth book in the series is due out soon.*

Johnnie Jacobson's hands gripped the handrims of his wheelchair so tightly, his knuckles turned white. Pushing his chair down a dirt driveway was no easy job. He could have used his crutches, but he thought wheeling would be easier. Now he wasn't so sure.

Johnnie, who was born with cerebral palsy, had good upper body strength. He could "walk" with the help of crutches, though it made him tired. Unlike people with more severe cerebral palsy, or CP as he called it, he could speak clearly and with only a slight slur. People usually commented on his bright smile and cheerful attitude. His parents and sisters also knew that behind those dark brown eyes was a lot of mischief. ...

A lot of Johnnie's positive attitude was a result of having a loving family. From the time Johnnie was little, his mother and father encouraged him to try new things. They never did for him what they knew he could do for himself. He learned how to ride a tricycle, swim, dive and play sports. Johnnie grew up believing there wasn't anything he couldn't do if he put his mind to it.

And right now Johnnie knew he had to put his mind to getting to that barn. Johnnie looked at the long, winding driveway, took a deep breath and nudged the wheels of his chair forward. As he trudged along, he was aware that his newfound friends were watching him. It was part of the initiation.

At one point, when he hit a rut in the road and had a hard time pushing past it, he muttered, "If it weren't for that kid — what's his name? Oh, yeah, Travis Hughes — the one with the big mouth — one of the other kids would have pushed me down to the barn. But, no! Travis didn't want me in the neighborhood club to begin with. He said,

"We don't want anyone in the Gun Lake Gang who can't hold his own." ...

Travis took one look at the leg braces, crutches and then the wheelchair and decided Johnnie was a "loser." It was only after the other kids in the club insisted on giving Johnnie a chance that Travis agreed to let him go through the initiation.

Johnnie had accepted the challenge with an "I'll-show-you" attitude. But now, here he was about halfway down the long, winding driveway heading toward the old abandoned barn, thinking that this initiation was more like "mission impossible." According to the rules of the initiation, he had to go into the barn and retrieve something to prove he had gone inside. Then and only then would he be allowed to become a member of the Gun Lake Gang. ...

Johnnie was tired from pushing his wheelchair. The long shadows stretching across the road encouraged his mind to remember all the ghost stories he had ever heard. With renewed determination, he gave his wheelchair a few more pushes toward the barn doors — only to discover they were locked.

Though he was tempted to give up, Travis' sharp words prodded him to find some way of getting inside. The other kids must have done it, he thought.

Johnnie inched along the side of the barn looking for loose boards or another door. As he rounded the corner to the back of the barn, his search was rewarded. Another set of barn doors greeted him — and they weren't nailed shut. However, a padlock secured a chain that was looped through the door handles. Frustrated, Johnnie grabbed the padlock, gritted his teeth and yanked it. To his surprise, the lock gave way. He quickly pulled the lock out of the chain and threw it to the ground. Then slowly, he opened the barn doors. ...

Reprinted with permission of Cedar Tree Publishing, 888-302-7463.

Nonfiction: A Dragon of a Topic

Here is a section from Disabilities, Dragons and Other Magical Discoveries: A Kid's Guide to Understanding and Living with Disabilities *(see page 104 to order). The section is called "Kidney and Bladder Function." Reprinted with permission.*

This is one of those topics that most people would rather not discuss. Going to the bathroom usually happens in private, so talking about it in public can be embarrassing. ... The good news is that we can talk about most of the embarrassing topics right away and get them over with! The bad news is that many people with chronic or disabling conditions need some help going to the bathroom.

Kidneys spend their whole life "taking out the garbage."

The blood that your heart pumps through your body carries oxygen and useful nutrients to all the cells of your body. It also carries away carbon dioxide and the waste products and chemicals that the cells don't use. Then, many times every day, the blood passes through the kidneys. There the waste products get removed, along with any extra water your body doesn't need right away.

There are two kidneys, and they send this waste liquid (called urine) down two short tubes (called ureters) to the bladder. The bladder is a bag made of muscle. Several times a day, the nerves in the muscle tell your brain that your bladder is full. Then, the muscles of the bladder squeeze or contract, and urine is forced out of the body through another tube called the urethra. The polite scientific term for this is urination. The common term is peeing.

People with neurological disabilities may have a condition called neurogenic bladder. This means the nerves from the bladder don't know that it's full, or the bladder doesn't contract and relax correctly. This can result in several different problems.

First, the bladder sphincter may not stay closed and urine can leak out. People with this problem may get wet with no warning. This is called incontinence. Sometimes medications can help reduce this problem by tightening the sphincter so that it stays closed.

The opposite problem can also occur when the sphincter is stuck shut. This can cause really serious problems. The inside of the bladder is warm, wet and dark, just the sort of place where bacteria love to gather and grow. This can cause urinary tract infections, Or U.T.I. The symptoms of a U.T.I. include high fever, strong smelling urine, and sometimes blood or pus in the urine. This needs treatment right away! Antibiotics are usually used to treat the infection.

If the urine backs up all the way to the kidneys, this is called reflux. Kidneys produce urine, but they are supposed to get rid of it right away, not swim in it! If they are exposed to urine for too long, cells in the kidney start to get sick or even die.

"Whew, that feels better."

Illustrations by Herb Regalo

A common treatment for reflux is called clean intermittent catheterization or C.I.C. Every few hours, a clean piece of plastic tubing is passed into the bladder, allowing the urine to empty out. Children as young as 3 or 4 years old can learn to do this themselves ...

Here are some things you can do to help out your kidneys:
• Drink lots of water or clear fluids (6-8 glasses a day).
• Catheterize and take medication on time.
• If you get a U.T.I., go to your doctor right away.

So, if you have bladder problems, don't ignore them. If you look after your kidneys, they will look after you.

"Thanks for taking care of me."

Teaching Schools to Be Cool

School can be fun or frustrating. Sometimes it's scary. It can teach you lessons you love and some you wish you didn't have to learn. But most of all, school should be fair to all students. *Kids on Wheels* spent a day at one of the best schools in the country for wheelchair users. It's not perfect, but Price Elementary is a good example of a public school trying to do the right things for kids with disabilities. How does your school measure up? If you think it could be better, talk to your parents about it. Let them know you want to be treated fairly. Together, you can teach schools to be cool.

Illustration by Doug Davis

Welcome to Price Elementary

Allison Holden likes school, but her teacher tells bad jokes. Like now, she's on the Internet to find information for a social studies report on the state of Colorado. Her teacher, Mr. Wytonovich, comes by and asks her, "What's your state?"

"Colorado," she says, because that's the state she's researching. If he looked at the computer screen, he could see it for himself. It's right there in front of him.

"I mean your state of mind," he says, and he walks away, laughing.

"See what I mean," she whispers. His jokes are pretty bad.

Allison is 11 years old and she's in fifth grade. She's shy, pretty, and uses a wheelchair because she has spina bifida. In her classroom her desk is a few inches higher than the other desks and she has wire shelves along one side instead of a desk drawer. But other than that, it's the same as everyone else's desk. Like everyone else at her school, Allison wears a uniform, a white or blue shirt and then khaki or blue pants or skirt.

Allison's classroom is huge, it's the size of a gym, and there are sometimes two or three classes being taught at one time. There are posters, globes, computers, book cases and house plants all over the place. One section of the room is where some kids go for help in reading or math. Allison's grades are good, As and Bs, but like a lot of kids at her school she does sometimes go for extra help in both reading and math.

Price Elementary, where Allison goes to school, is a grade school for kids who are interested in arts and theater. So the school's run differently than other grade schools in the district. Sometimes artists come and teach classes in pottery, painting and quilting (the school is in Lancaster, Pennsylvania, which is world-famous for its quilts). There's even a fish pond in the school's lobby — the third graders got to pick out the fish.

Allison likes school — except for her teacher's bad jokes!

The school is almost completely wheelchair accessible. The school bus with a lift drops Allison and other kids who use wheelchairs off in the parking lot and, since there are no steps at the entrance, they come through the front door. Only one door is not wheelchair accessible — the fire drill door. All of the kids who use wheelchairs have to be carried outside every time there's a fire drill, usually by their aide and one of the teachers.

Even though the fire drill door has steps, Price is still the most wheelchair accessible elementary school in Lancaster. For that reason, all the kids who use wheelchairs in that area attend Price. They don't all go to the same classes, they don't all have the same teacher, and they're not all in the same grade. In fact, they're very different from each other.

The kids who use wheelchairs do have some things in common, though.

They all have an aide who works only with them. Each aide does different things for each kid, but most aides help the kids open up their lunches, go to the bathroom, write down notes or assignments, let the teacher know when they want to answer a question, and reach things that are too high or stuck in corners. When kids are in first, second and third grade, their aides do a lot for them — the aides even help them do their homework. In Lancaster, junior high starts with sixth grade, so once the kids grow older and are getting ready to go to junior high, the aides don't help with their schoolwork as much, and instead just help with the other stuff.

Allison's aide is Mrs. Carter. "I was told by the principle to give Allison more independence this year, to get ready for middle school," says Mrs. Carter. "Now she soars on her own." Last year, Mrs. Carter helped Allison with her assignments. "I was there for every moment, and this year, she's like, 'I got it,' she's doing the assignment on states by herself."

"When you grow up you might not have an aide," says Allison. "You'll have to be independent. But I'm not scared."

Bats, Thugs and Lightbulbs

Matt Wagner's aide, Shar, is cool. First, she lets him call her "Shar," even though she's a grown-up and he's only in the fifth grade. Second, she lets him pick on her sometimes. He says that, like Mr. Wytonovich, Shar's jokes aren't funny. "And when she sings in the elevator, *oh my word!* She needs lessons," says Matt. Matt prefers Ozzy Osborne's singing to Shar's. Ozzy Osborne is an old rock star from years ago who was famous for wearing lots of makeup and biting the heads off of real live bats. Matt's a big Ozzy fan, and whenever he's bored, he pretends to

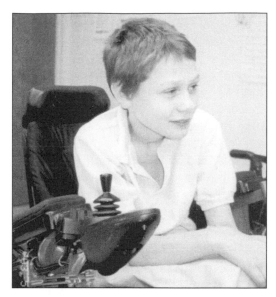

Whenever Matt gets bored, he pretends to bite off bat heads like Ozzy Osbourne.

bite off bat heads.

Shar and Matt like each other a whole lot and Shar helps Matt out whenever he needs it. "She helps me get my books out, helps me write sometimes, helps with lunch," says Matt. "And sometimes she helps me in the bathroom." Matt goes to the nurse's office a couple of times a day to use the bathroom. He can do almost everything in the bathroom himself, like, he can catherize himself, but still needs help with some other things. Matt has been quadriplegic ever since a gun accident five years ago, and for him that means he can move his arms and hands a little bit but he can't move his legs.

"I'm not uncomfortable going to the bathroom at school," he says. He's more embarrassed when he drops pens or papers in class and Shar has to pick them up for him. He sometimes feel as if the other kids make fun of him when that happens. He doesn't get picked on, but some of the other kids are what he calls, "the mafia." Shar calls them "wanna-be thugs."

When Matt came back to school after being in the hospital from October to December he was far behind, even though he tried to do a lot of his work from the hospital. "It's hard because some of the stuff you can't do and then you just don't feel like doing it anymore," he says. "Like my science project, Shar keeps pushing it." For his project he wired a light bulb into a potato, and then waited to see what would happen.

Surgeries and Schoolwork

Like Matt, many kids who use wheelchairs spend weeks or months during the school year in hospitals. Allison also spends a lot of time in hospitals, and so does her friend, Kia Phillips. Kia has cerebral palsy, which for her means she can walk a little bit with a walker and she has trouble using one of her hands and arms. She uses a wheelchair, too, when she's tired of the walker. Kia is 10, she's not shy at all, she's in the fourth grade and she has a very pretty smile.

"It's sad, because I want to learn what they're learning, too, but I can't be there," says Kia, about being in the hospital during the school year. Like Allison, she's smart and gets good grades, but sometimes needs help with reading and math. Matt needs help with reading sometimes, but he finally got caught up in math and now math's his favorite subject.

Kia says it's hard to catch up on school work after surgeries.

It's hard to keep up with your classmates when you miss so much of the school year. "You feel left out," says Kia.

Most recently, Kia's had surgeries on

her hands and legs. "Surgeries aren't worth it because you still can't do what you want to do," says Kia. "Coming back to school is kind of tough because you've got to get used to where your surgery is and it hurts."

Kia's aide, Mrs. Dunn, mostly just helps Kia in the lunchroom and the bathroom. "I get a little bit shy about that, but I got used to it," says Kia, about being helped in the bathroom. During lunchtime, Mrs. Dunn opens up Kia's lunch so that Kia won't use her teeth. Mrs. Dunn also helps her reach stuff in the classroom that's in the corners and other places that you can't get to easily if you use a wheelchair or walker.

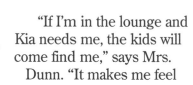

"If I'm in the lounge and Kia needs me, the kids will come find me," says Mrs. Dunn. "It makes me feel good, I love coming to school." The other kids fought over who gets to help Kia and Mrs. Dunn, so now Mrs. Dunn has a place on the helper wall called "Mrs. Dunn's Helper" and the kids take turns.

"Last year I was writing for Kia, sharpening her pencils and stuff like that," says Mrs. Dunn. "But I was told by our principle that Kia needs to learn to be more independent." So this year, Kia does as much for herself as she can.

Kia has lots of friends at her school. "The other kids think my wheelchair is cool," she says. "I say to them, 'I'll trade you.'" Sometimes she'll let them ride in it and they think that's fun.

Although Kia smiles and laughs a lot, she sometimes feels blue. "I cheer her up when she's down, tell her my sob stories," says Mrs. Dunn. "I was looked down on in school because of my height." She's shorter than most of the fifth grade kids, even though she's a grown-up.

"It doesn't matter if you're short," Kia tells Mrs. Dunn. "You're still my best friend."

Things Kids Hate

The Price Elementary playground has all of the usual stuff — swings, sliding boards, a jungle gym and kids playing ball games. But it doesn't have anything fun for kids who can't run or catch. So for Allison, Matt and Kia, recess stinks. It's not much fun sitting there watching everyone else have a good time.

Since there's nothing else to do, Kia walks or wheels around the playground until the bell rings, or stays inside and draws flowers. "I'd like to climb a jungle gym," she says. "I could try, but the other kids are too wild." Mrs. Dunn did help her into a toddler swing, once. That helped kill some time.

Matt loves physical activity and takes part in the Special Olympics. In fact, at the Special Olympics he shoots a bow

Continued on page 114

P.E. and Recess

Most schools fall short when it comes to adapting gym class. There are a couple of things you can do: First, explore adaptive recreation organizations outside of your school (see Chapter 2). Second, bring some of the things you learn there back to your school. For example, you might not be able to play stand-up basketball, but if the school collected some used wheelchairs, everyone could play wheelchair basketball. Or maybe the school can change its gym class activities to include sports that can be played from a wheelchair, such as tennis.

Recess is also a common problem because most playgrounds aren't accessible. If your school is planning to rebuild its playground, get involved in the process. Teach the planners about "universal design" that allows all kids access to playground equipment (see page 56).

Beth Kolbe: Going Back to School – and Life – after Injury

Ever since the car accident that left her quadriplegic, Beth Kolbe and her friends laugh at the strangest things. Like once in choir class Beth's friend, Jackie, accidentally knocked her off of the big, carpeted step they were sitting on. "And Jackie just sat there and laughed," says Beth. "My choir teacher pretty much freaked out at first, and he got me back into my chair really fast. It was great."

Beth's glad her friends aren't weird about her disability. Her accident happened the summer before ninth grade and her friends helped her a lot that year. "I had a really close friend in each class who knew about my leg spasms," she says. "Now I have that under control, but for the first year they would help with spasms and carry my books. They still help me with my books because it's more fun that way."

At first her friends took notes for her, too, and she'd sometimes have her parents write down what she said for long writing assignments. "But I don't have to do that anymore, which is good." She learned that if she tilts her wrists up she can write pretty well. "It took awhile for my teachers to be able to read my handwriting," she says.

Beth is the first student at Columbian High School to use a wheelchair and at first her teachers were cautious, especially during fire drills when they had to carry her down stairs. "They would all freak out like, 'OK now, if we touch her are we going to break her?' It took a while for them to realize I don't break."

Now her school has an elevator, a ramp, electric doors, "and

Illustration by Doug Davis

they gave me my own little room for the bathroom, which was really cool," says Beth. "It has a locker-type thing and a bathroom, too." And the school added an electric platform to its stadium so she can go up into the bleachers and watch football games with her friends.

One of the worst things about going back to school after her accident was using the bathroom. "For the first two years my mom came to do my bladder stuff everyday at lunch," says Beth. "But then I got bladder surgery so

I can do it on my own." Because of the surgery, Beth just has to reach her stomach to be able to catherize herself through a port in her abdomen.

Before her injury she never thought about what she wanted to do after high school, "but I've become more interested in medicine as a job since my injury. I love biology and anything with cells and the small stuff." She thought about being a doctor, but says she's been in enough hospitals to know she wouldn't want to work in one all the time. Since she wants to go into medicine Beth's grades are very important to her and for three years in a row she got all As.

She has this advice to other kids who have spinal cord injuries: "Don't change your plans just because of something that happened to you, keep doing what you've always wanted to do. Don't let anything change it." For example, even though she can't be on the volleyball team anymore, she can still swim, and she competes against other people who use wheelchairs from around the nation. "I'm trying to get to the Paralympics," she says. "In my last swim meet I broke an American record and they announced it during morning announcements in my school, so that was kind of cool."

Alex Caldwell: Future President of the United States?

Fifth-grader Alex Caldwell says his ultimate goal in life is to be president of the United States of America. To practice running a campaign, Alex ran for student council. "My motto was 'fishing for your vote' and I passed out the cheese snack fish things," he says. He didn't win, but says he'll try again.

If he's not elected president when he grows up, Alex will settle for being a lawyer. "I might want to be president in the future, but if I don't make it to president that's OK, law is interesting to me."

What kind of lawyer does he want to be? "I want to be a criminal prosecutor because I think people should be punished if they do a crime and I want to help with that," he says. "But it wasn't so much prosecution that interested me. I wanted to be a lawyer because I heard most presidents are lawyers first."

Also, prosecutors get to figure out problems — like, how to prove the guy on trial is guilty — which makes law a lot like math. And math is Alex' all-time favorite subject. "Right now we're doing fractions and I enjoy that. I've always gotten As and Bs," says Alex. "I like math because it's always been pretty easy."

Alex goes to Gables Elementary School in Columbus, Ohio, and uses a wheelchair for his spina bifida. He gets great grades in all his classes, not just math, and he doesn't get extra help in any of his subjects. Of course, Alex passed all five parts of the Ohio proficiency test and he scored "honors" in three areas, including math, and on his last report card he got all As.

"Grades are important to me because I want to go to college so I can go to law school," says Alex. "I figure if I start getting good grades now then I'll do good in high school, and that's probably where they really start paying attention."

and arrow. But the gym class at school doesn't have anything he can do, so instead he says he does nothing during gym class, "I just watch."

And, even though the school plans neat field trips, the places they go aren't always accessible. Like, once, they all went to the Gettysburg battlefield, and everyone went into the battlefield's buildings but the kids who use wheelchairs. They just kind of sat around the door, trying to look inside and see all the cool Civil War costumes.

But Allison's biggest pet peeve has nothing to do with boring gym classes, dumb recesses or dopey inaccessible field trips. Instead, her biggest peeve is other kids who jump in front of her when she's going down the hall at school. Kids who walk always think they go faster than kids who roll, and that's not true. All they do is get on the nerves of the kids who roll. And Allison, even though she's usually shy and quiet, can only take other kids getting on her nerves for so long.

"Allison gears it up when people cut in front of her and then, WHAM," says Mrs. Carter. She slams her wheelchair into the back of some line-cutter's legs.

"Yup," says Allison, with a big smile.

"I hate it when people cut in front of me, too," adds Kia.

Matt drives a huge power chair that lets him lean back, raises so he's as tall as the other kids, and drives like a tank. Not even the wanna-be thugs cut in front of him. While the girls discuss the best strategies for tripping kids who cut in front of them, Matt just leans back and pretends to bite off bat heads.

The Future

In Social Studies, Matt sits tall in his powerchair, one kid in a wide circle of kids sitting around a VCR. His teacher, Mr. Beamer, tells all of them to pretend they have $1 million to plan a road trip anywhere, to do anything. But they have to figure out what they'll drive, where they'll stay, and what roads they'll take. To help, Mr. Beamer has a videotape of a road trip he took last summer and in it he explains a lot about how he decided where to go and how he got there.

This is Matt's last year in elementary school. Getting ready for a new school is a lot like planning that imaginary road trip for Mr. Beamer, only without the million dollars or a helpful videotape. Matt knows where he's going — next year he's going to junior high and then high school, and then he wants to go on to college. And he knows what he needs to do to get there — keep getting good grades.

Matt wants to study computers in college and be a video game designer when he grows up, and so even when it's not easy because he's doing his work from a hospital again or because he's afraid he'll never catch up or because he needs help from an aide, he works hard on his schoolwork. It shows on his report card, he mostly gets As and Bs.

Even though sometimes he thinks he'd rather not work so hard, Matt says the trick to getting where he wants to go is to never quit. "Don't give up, ever," Matt says. "If I give up I'll never meet my dreams." 🦎

JOSIE BYZEK is an editor for New Mobility *magazine and has had multiple sclerosis since she was a teenager. She lives in Lancaster, Pa., with her four cats, two turtles, one tarantula and various human family members.*

Don't keep your friends in the dark

To order more copies of Kids on Wheels, have parents, teachers or therapists call

888-850-0344, ext. 209

KIDS ON WHEELS

Making Friends, Fitting In, Standing Out

I still remember my first day of middle school. As I wheeled my chair to my first class, I noticed how all the other kids towered over me. In elementary school I had been just one of a hundred kids who used wheelchairs. I had done well in my classes, I had been popular, and in my final year I had served as student body president. But now? I couldn't even look my fellow students in the eye without giving myself a stiff neck. They ran at top speed down the halls, they shoved each other out of the way. Girls' purses smacked me in the back of the head as I tried to keep up with the crowd. Boys bumped into my wheelchair and then glared at me, as if it were my fault that they didn't watch where they were going. I felt small, invisible.

At the end of the day, I told my mom tearfully that I wanted to go to the "special" school instead.

Gently, my mom encouraged me to be patient and give my new school a chance. She reminded me of how much I had hated not going to the same elementary school as my nondisabled brothers and sister. "Everyone feels scared and lost at a new school," she said. "But soon you'll make new friends, try new things, and become more confident. Before you know it you'll be wondering what you had to be scared of."

The author when he was 8 years old.

> "I realized that most of the other kids were just as nervous about talking to me as I was about talking to them."

It took longer than we both thought it would, and it wasn't easy, but my mom was right. I loved both writing and music, so I joined the school newspaper and played clarinet in the band. After a while, I realized that most of the other kids were just as nervous about talking to me as I was about talking to them. Even some of those who teased me at first eventually became lifelong friends.

When I was in sixth grade, kids with disabilities usually went to separate, "special" schools. Putting us in the same classrooms as nondisabled kids — called "mainstreaming" back then — was a new and controversial idea. Nowadays, however, the law guarantees your right to equal treatment, and it is far more common for disabled kids to attend the same schools as everyone else. (Now the word for it is "inclusion.")

friends

Making new friends is still hard, though. Being the only kid around who uses a wheelchair can make it even harder. But it's not impossible. After all, your wheelchair lets you go places you wouldn't be able to reach otherwise. If you want to be popular and feel good about yourself, it can take you there, too.

Illustrations by Doug Davis

Self-Esteem and Social Life

Here's a little secret: Even some adults have a tough time meeting new people. If you sit back and watch adults at a party, you'll notice that the way they act isn't really much different from the way kids do. Some of them will jump right in and introduce themselves to everyone in the room. Others are shy and will stand quietly against the wall, speaking only when other people come up to them. For both kids and adults, how easily they deal with social situations has a lot to do with what is called *self-esteem*.

Self-esteem is the way that you feel about yourself. It comes from within you, but can be made better or worse by the people or things that happen around you. Do you believe that you're a likeable person who can do a lot of things well and handle any situation? If so, your self-esteem would be considered very high. People with low self-esteem don't believe many others like them. They have little or no confidence in their own abilities and are afraid that if they try anything new, they'll fail. If your self-esteem is high, chances are that making new friends comes easily and naturally to you. Low self-esteem, meanwhile, can make it very hard even to talk to someone you don't know. For Cassandra Saunders, who has cerebral palsy, self-esteem and making friends go hand in hand. "It was high when I had friends, but when I didn't have friends it was very low."

Having a disability can have a powerful effect on your self-esteem. You see people around you doing all sorts of things that you can't do, and it can make you feel worthless. Rude or ignorant remarks from other kids and adults can also make it seem as if no one likes you. But being disabled doesn't have to give

Tatyana McFadden (front) boosts her self-esteem with sports and physical activity (see her profile, page 51). And friends? Well, they just fall in line!

you a low opinion of yourself. Remember, you have strengths and abilities that others don't. And the ways you have adapted to the challenges of living in the world of the nondisabled should also be a source of pride.

So how do you raise your own self-esteem?

• Look for activities that you like to do. The more you enjoy an activity, the more likely you are to do it well. And the better your performance, the more capable you feel, and the prouder you are of your achievements.

• Keep in mind that you are unique. Don't spend too much time comparing yourself with other kids. You may not be able to run around the playground, but you may be able to read faster, or do better at math. Everyone has different strengths and weaknesses.

• Don't try too hard to be what you believe others want you to be. Alex Caldwell, a 12-year-old with spina bifida, says, "It doesn't matter what other people think — what matters is what you think of yourself."

Still, even with high self-esteem, you may have trouble "breaking the ice" in a new school or social situation. This is normal, whether or not you have a disability. Here are a few things you can do to meet new people and help them get to know you:

• Join school clubs and organizations that you're interested in. If you like computers, for example, joining your school's computer club will put you together with other kids who share your interests.

• Go to school dances, parties, sports events, and so on. Even if you can't dance or don't care about sports, you can still have a good time.

• Be interested in other people. Ask them about their favorite movies, their pets, anything that excites them. Other kids — and adults — love talking about themselves, and they'll start viewing you more and more as a friend if they know that you're interested in who they are.

• Don't feel as if you constantly have to be the center of attention. Nobody likes someone who interrupts others when they're talking, bosses them around, and always has to get his or her way. Having a social life is about participating in a group, not dominating it.

Illustration by Doug Davis

Above all, BE YOURSELF. The best friends you will ever make in your life are those who know the real person that you are.

Explaining Your Disability

I was born with a condition called osteogenesis imperfecta — OI, for short (also known as "brittle bones"). As a kid I spent a lot of time in the hospital recovering from broken bones or surgery. My parents and I worried that the nurses and hospital staff might accidentally hurt me if they weren't aware of my condition. So, we eventually got a piece of yellow poster board, wrote "FRAGILE" on it with a black felt-tip pen, and taped it above my hospital bed. That was all the explanation anybody needed.

Human beings are naturally curious — and they aren't always polite about how they express it. As a kid with a disability, you see that every day. People stare at you as you wheel around the mall. They ask questions about you or your chair. It can be very frustrating to deal with. But it's also important to remember that these people don't mean to be rude or to hurt your feelings. They've just never seen anyone like you before, and they want to find out about you. Being rude back to them only makes matters worse.

Nadia Roberts, now 15, also has OI. At her school, other kids sometimes avoid her at first, fearing that they might do something that causes a broken bone. "I just tell them that it's cool — that my wheels are my legs," she says. "I just try to make the other kids comfortable with me." Her 8-year-old brother Steven, who also has OI, says he makes friends by "just being nice, and helping them." If one of the other kids falls on the playground, Steven checks to make sure he or she is OK, just as they should do for him.

Whatever your disability happens to be — OI, cerebral palsy, muscular dystrophy, whatever — being open to questions helps other people to get over their nervousness around you. Sometimes, making a joke about it works well — I often tell people that my bones "have the consistency of an English muffin" — while at other times a serious approach is better. The important thing, though, is to be honest. Cassandra tells people, "I'm just as normal as everybody else. I just have to sit all the time."

When Kids Tease

"Back in kindergarten," Alex says, "there was one kid who used to call me 'Wheelchair Boy.' That really got to me

Photo by Mark Courtney/Star News

for a while. I told the teachers about it, and they talked to him, and he eventually apologized."

When I first started middle school, one boy used to come up to me every day at lunch and say, "You look like a space alien." I tried to ignore him, then I tried to avoid him, but that just seemed to egg him on. So I finally turned around and told him, "That's right — I am a space alien. You'd better be careful, or I'll call my ship and have them abduct you." He never bothered me again after that.

It's unfortunate, but teasing is a part of life when you're a kid. Kids can be very cruel to each other, and especially to those who are different. You're all at a period in your lives when you're still learning about yourselves — and some of you try to do that by tearing down and hurting others. So how can you deal with the bullies in your life?

• Don't react with anger. That's the sort of response a bully wants. It's not easy to do sometimes, but try to ignore him or her if you can.

• Make a joke out of it. A good sense of humor can often help to ease a tense situation.

• If things turn physical and you start to feel threatened, tell a parent or teacher about it. Teasing may be a part of life, but you have the right to protect yourself. No one should have to feel unsafe at school.

The good news is, school doesn't last forever. After you graduate, any name-calling or bullying you have suffered will become a distant memory. As for now, keep in mind that those kids who tease you are really just as insecure about themselves as you are. And they — like you — are always changing. It's possible that those same kids will end up becoming your closest friends later on.

When Adults Freeze

A few years ago, one of my old friends revealed something to me. He said that on the first day I came to their school, his homeroom teacher made an announcement to the class. "We have a new student this year — a boy in a wheelchair," the teacher told them. "Be nice to him, because he only has a couple of years left to live."

It wasn't true. I was just as likely to survive the next two years as anyone else at that school. To this day I have no idea if my friend's teacher actually believed I was going to die, or simply lied to the class so they wouldn't pick on me. But either way, it goes to show that adults can act weird around disabled kids, too.

Nadia says, "One time during recess, I got hit by a ball and hurt my finger.

The teachers freaked out. I had to tell them it was nothing and not to call my parents. Every little thing that happens to me, they call my parents."

Just because someone is older than you doesn't mean they know more than you do about being disabled. It's possible that they know even less than your nondisabled classmates. (After all, when many adults were your age, disabled people were often kept apart from the rest of society, in institutions or "special" schools.) And if that's the case, they may also be afraid to ask questions. So, it might be up to you to help educate them. Try breaking the ice with a simple question of your own, like, "Is there anything you'd like to know about me?" Chances are good that they mean well, but they think that you'll be insulted if they ask about your wheelchair. Alex says, "I don't like being treated differently by adults, but I try not to say anything that will hurt their feelings."

Yes, adults have feelings too.

Saying No

We all want to impress our friends. Being well-liked and fitting in with

Real friends don't try to force you to do things that are dangerous just to be popular.

Illustration by Doug Davis

My Chair Is Not a Toy

You're the only kid who uses a wheelchair at your school, and the other kids just love to play around with it. They stick things in the spokes, they pop wheelies with you in it, they come up behind you and push you when you don't want them to. Maybe they're just teasing. Maybe they've never seen a wheelchair before and are curious about how it works. Or maybe they think you have trouble getting around and just want to help. All you know is that they can't seem to keep their hands off of it, and you want them to stop.

I once got so frustrated with kids playing with my wheelchair that my brother and I decided to electrify it. We would run wires from the handles down the back of the chair and attach them to a 9-volt battery hidden in my backpack. Then, if one of the kids at school grabbed the handles, he or she would get a small electrical shock and hopefully learn not to do it again.

It would have worked. We even drew up plans for it. But then I mistakenly left the plans out where one of the teachers saw it, and I got sent to the counselor's office for a talking-to about the dangers of electricity. So much for that idea.

After a while, though, I learned that I didn't have to physically hurt my classmates to get them to stop playing with my chair. If you're having the same problem, the key is to be firm, but polite.

Illustration by Doug Davis

Acting rude or upset almost always backfires. If the other kids are trying to tease you, they've succeeded in getting a reaction from you. And if they just want to help, in the future they might be scared of helping you even when you need it.

Yet at the same time, you depend on your wheelchair to get from place to place—it's almost a part of your body. And you have the right to expect it to be treated that way. If your nondisabled classmates don't get the idea, explain it to them this way: "If I kept grabbing your legs while you were trying to walk down the hall, you wouldn't like it, would you?"

the group seem especially important when you're a kid. And if you're the only kid in the group who uses a wheelchair, you may feel you need to prove that you can do anything the others can. But remember, real friends don't try to force you to do things that are dangerous just to be popular.

Your parents may have once told you something like, "If everyone else is jumping off a cliff, that doesn't mean you have to jump too." I actually did jump off a cliff once, for that very reason. It still hurts when I think about it.

When I was about 7 years old, I went to the park with my brother and his friends. They were the only nondisabled kids I hung out with at the time, and I desperately wanted them to like me. At one end of the park there was a hill, which rose gradually on one side and dropped off sharply on the other. The whole group walked up the hill, with me wheeling along behind them, trying to keep up. As they reached the top, each of them jumped up in the air and went sliding down the steep slope on the other side. Finally, I was the only one left

friends

Be a Winner!

Are you the only wheelchair user you know? Do you want to meet other kids who also use chairs and know what it's like? Winners on Wheels might be just the group for you.

Modeled after groups like the Boy Scouts and Girl Scouts, WOW is made up of wheelchair-using kids between the ages of 6 and 18. Like members of those other organizations, WOW members meet in small groups — called "circles" — take part in a lot of different activities, and earn merit badges, or "wheels," as they learn new skills. Some of the wheels are for fun — bowling, hockey, nature — while others involve community service, personal safety and building self-esteem. Taking part in WOW is a great way not only to make new friends, but also to become more independent and be more successful in anything you want to do.

Right now there are 21 WOW circles around the country, with more forming in the future. To find out more, you can check them out on the Web at www.wowusa.com.

at the top of the hill.

"Come on, Doug!" the others said to me. "Come on down! It's not far."

"No," I said. "It's too steep."

"Come on, don't be a chicken! If you fall down, we'll catch you."

I hesitated a little longer, but then gave into the pressure and pushed my chair down the hill. I was right the first time — it was too steep. One of my front wheels got caught on a rock and I tipped over, tumbling to the bottom. My next trip was to the hospital with two broken legs.

After that, I learned to stick up for myself and to listen to my instincts. If my instincts told me something was stupid or dangerous, I knew that it was OK to say no. I got teased for it at first, but my friends soon came to respect me — because I didn't put myself in danger just to get others to like me.

Birds of a Feather

When I was mainstreamed into the "normal" school, I avoided the one or two other disabled kids who went there. It was more important to me that I be accepted by the nondisabled kids. "I'd better stay away from those cripples," I said to myself. "People might think that I'm a cripple too."

That was a big mistake on my part. By looking down

my nose at other disabled kids, I was only hurting my own self-esteem. I may not have wanted anyone to think of me as just "The Kid in the Wheelchair," but I shouldn't have been ashamed of it either.

Nadia understands better than I did how important it is to include disabled kids in her circle of friends. "I enjoy being around other kids in wheelchairs," she says. "I know one boy named Caleb—he races, he plays basketball, stuff that I like to do. With other kids, they get afraid that I'm going to get hurt. But when I'm with wheelchair kids, I just do whatever they do." Alex agrees: "It seems like we have more to talk about. We have more things in common."

Even if you are the only wheelchair user at your school, you are still part of a larger community. There are millions of us just in the United States. We have our own sports teams, our own scout troops, and our own newspapers and magazines. There are people who use wheelchairs in Congress, in the boardrooms of large corporations, in the movies, and on television. If you put us all together in one place — say, in the biggest, most wheelchair-accessible stadium in the world — we would have a lot to say to each other. We would laugh at many of the same jokes and talk about all the weird things nondisabled people have said to us.

But of course, if we spent all of our time there, we wouldn't be part of the rest of the world.

So, by all means, be part of that world. Enjoy the company of your friends, whether they're disabled or not. But also remember that you are not alone. 🏃

DOUG LATHROP is an editor of New Mobility, *a lifestyle magazine for adult wheelchair users. He was born with osteogenesis imperfecta and attended nondisabled school from seventh grade until graduation. He lives in San Diego, California.*

Would you like to see a color MAGAZINE called

Kids on Wheels?

Visit us on the Web at

www.kidsonwheels.us

and let us know what you think!

family

By Ben Mattlin

The Strength of Families

Every kid has a family, but no two families are alike. Some kids live with their mom and dad, others live with Mom but see Dad only sometimes or live with Dad and see Mom only sometimes. Still other kids live with grandparents, aunts or uncles. Brothers and sisters are parts of families, too.

Not all families have a kid who uses a wheelchair. That's part of what makes your family unique.

Families help one another. Does your mom or dad wake you up in the morning and get you to school? Does your brother or sister play with you? And someone makes sure there's food to eat for dinner, even if it's broccoli, right?

Families help in other ways, too.

"My parents hug me a lot to make me feel loved, and it helps me heal from things that happen during my school day," says Amy Litzinger, 14, who lives in Austin, Texas. Amy uses a power wheelchair because she has cerebral palsy, which comes from a brain injury at birth. "I have no sitting or standing balance," she says, "but my vision, hearing, speaking and intelligence are fine."

Everybody knows there are good parts and not-so-good good parts about family life. Sometimes you have to do things you don't want to do.

"My parents don't expect many

"Naomi has definitely made everyone in our family more sensitive, understanding and patient," says 12-year-old Amber Catford-Robinson about her sister. "Our family is pretty close, too, because there have been major surgeries and times when we didn't know if she would live or die." (See Naomi's profile, page 14.)

chores because I can't do many," Amy says. Well, that's definitely one of the good things about Amy's family life!

Illustration by Doug Davis

Family Fun

Besides helping one another with chores, families play together. A lot of families like to play board games like Monopoly. Others watch sports together and root for their favorites. Family fun is important, so it's good to find fun activities that everyone can enjoy.

Amy

Most kids in wheelchairs like to play with their dolls or toy cars, watch TV, go to movies, play on their computers, and read stories — just like all kids. Many enjoy swimming, camping, singing (in a church choir, for instance), and accessible sports such as adaptive skiing or wheelchair basketball. These days, whatever your interest there's probably some way kids on wheels can participate too! (See Chapters 2 and 3.)

Amy loves doing Girl Scouts with her mother. "My mom is the group leader, so our activities are always accessible. Once, we put on a Disability Awareness Fair and 2,000 people came!"

Amy has 73 merit badges from the Girl Scouts.

For many kids, there's nothing better than just going to the park — especially if the park has an accessible playground with ramps so kids in wheelchairs can roll onto the play structures. In Los Angeles, one company was created just to help build more wheelchair-friendly playgrounds across the country. It's called Shane's Inspiration. You can learn more about it and other accessible playgrounds on page 56.

Theme parks are another fun family activity. Anna Lennartson, an 11-year-old girl in Round Rock, Texas, who was born with osteogenesis imperfecta, or brittle-bone disorder, is thankful for the Make-A-Wish Foundation (www.wish.org or 800-722-9474) because it "sent me on a trip to Disney World, which my family would never have been able to afford."

Not all rides are wheelchair accessible, but kids in wheelchairs usually get to skip the lines at Disneyland and Disney World. "What a wonderful way to go!" says Mary Robinson in upstate New York, whose daughter Megan, 12, uses a wheelchair sometimes. "To the front of those lines, no questions asked! We also found that hanging an old backpack on the back of Meg's chair made a wonderful carry-all bag for all of us."

Remember: Your Parents Love You ...

"Sometimes my parents won't let me do certain things because they're afraid it will be too rough. They don't think it's safe," says Anna.

Anna's story is probably familiar to many children with disabilities. How does it make you feel when your parents say "No"?

Even if you understand that your mom and dad probably have a good reason for saying no — like Anna's parents — it can still make you sad and angry. It's hard to imagine it as an expression of love.

Love?

Yes, because love means caring. If your parents didn't care about you, they would let you do anything you want. They wouldn't care if you did something dangerous. They wouldn't care if you got hurt.

Another way of expressing love is just being there day after day to help. Many kids who use wheelchairs rely on their mom or dad to help them get dressed in the morning, to feed them meals, and to help them with bathroom stuff.

That's love, too.

Anna knows it's true. "A lot of times I can't reach things or open doors. For certain automatic doors I'm too short to trigger the automatic opener, and I have to wait there for my mom to come," says Anna.

Parents come to your rescue all the time. 13-year-old Jenny Horsley in Jackson, Alabama, was born with a type of mitochondrial disease, which means she has weak muscles and little energy. She says that when other people stare at her or ask embarrassing questions about her disability, she turns to Mom for help. "It makes me feel very sad and I cry," says Jenny. "I don't know what to say, and then I look at my mom and she helps me."

... But They Get Tired

Jenny also feels a little sorry for her mom, especially on days when Jenny needs the most help from her. "My mom could use someone to help around the house," Jenny says. "She helps me all the time."

In Golden Valley, Minnesota, Wyatt Crouch is "one of the happiest kids I have ever met," says his mom. Wyatt, 4, uses a wheelchair almost all the time and cannot say words and sentences. "He smiles for yes and frowns for no, and I know through his pitch and tone if he's happy or sad," Wyatt's mom explains.

Wyatt gets "a lot more attention" than his twin 2-year-old sisters because he needs it. He also gets away with things they never will. "We don't tell him to stop playing with food or splashing water all over the bathroom floor," says

Wyatt's mom. "We consider most things he does to be a form of therapy."

Sound good? Well, just because Wyatt's parents let him make a mess doesn't mean they like it. After all, they are the ones who have to clean it up! And like all parents, sometimes they get tired of cleaning up their children's messes.

You might not see your parents' frustration. But you can tell when they're tired. And sometimes what makes parents tired is helping their children.

Parents may wish they didn't have to spend so much time or use so much energy helping a child who has a disability. You probably wish they didn't either. You and your parents have that in common. So you can probably understand when your mom seems less than cheerful about helping, or your dad grumbles about needing a rest. Even if it makes you feel bad.

Wyatt goes fishing with Uncle Bret.

It doesn't mean they don't love you. In fact, it means they do! To help somebody even when tired or frustrated is definitely an act of love. To show you love *them*, try to say "thanks" and be understanding.

Tips

One way that Wyatt's parents show their love — and their understanding of his situation — is by helping his teachers and friends at school better understand Wyatt's rare disability. Every year they buy a copy of a favorite book called *It's Okay to Be Different,* by Todd Parr, for Wyatt's classroom. "The book shows a little boy in a wheelchair," his mother

family

explains. She says he gets very excited when the teacher reads it to his class.

What's one of your favorite books? Wouldn't you like to share it with your class? It's a great way to tell people about yourself, or at least your taste in books! Discuss the idea with your parents and they are sure to agree. If all goes well, don't forget to say thank you. Or if you have a favorite book at school, tell your parents about it. Sharing books is a great way of letting people know you love them.

It's also a good idea to try to make good use of the times you share with your parents. If possible, don't spend all your together-time getting dressed, brushing teeth, and doing other necessary but boring tasks. "I don't go shopping with my mom anymore," says Jenny. "She goes while my nurse is here, so we can just go and have fun."

It might sound obvious, but try to talk openly and honestly with your parents. If you have questions about your disability, ask them. Or if you want to tell them about something that happened to you, or how you feel about the way they or other people treat you, go ahead.

Don't forget: Nobody knows better about how you feel than you do. Chances are your parents will welcome any news from you about how you feel or how you would like to be treated. After all, they can't read your mind. And don't be embarrassed to be honest, because there's nothing shameful about your feelings.

Brothers and Sisters

Most of the time Wyatt likes his twin 2-year-old sisters Dina and Bianca, but sometimes they bug him.

If you have brothers or sisters, you know how they can be pests sometimes. Are you ever a pest to them?

All brothers and sisters have fights, no matter how much they love each other. If you have a disability, the situation gets even more complicated.

"My parents try not to treat me differently from my sister, but a lot of things have to be different because I don't have the strength to do a lot," says Jenny. Jenny has a 17-year-old sister named Brittany.

Of course, playing with your brother or sister can be fun. "Sometimes they want me to go out and jump off the tree with them or do other crazy rough stuff that I can't do," groans Anna, who has brittle-bone disorder. Anna has had more than 40 broken bones in her life. (Not all at once, thank goodness!) She has twin 6-year-old brothers.

"They don't understand about my brittle bones," she says. "They don't understand that they can't be really rough with me. But at other times they think I'm going to break a bone if I do something simple, like swing really high."

Views from our Shoes

A book that can help you and your siblings understand each other is *Views from our Shoes: Growing Up with a Brother or Sister with Special Needs*. Lots of kids from age 4 to 18 write about what it's like to be the sibling with*out* a disability. Each writer talks about what's frustrating and what's great about their relationships. One of the things that comes out is how much brothers and sisters love each other — no matter what. *Views from our Shoes* is available in bookstores and on Amazon.com.

Understanding Their Frustrations

Many older brothers and sisters get jealous when a new baby is born. Babies need lots of attention, especially from Mom — attention that feels like it's being taken away from the older child, even though it's just a different kind of attention.

Kids in wheelchairs need lots of extra attention, too. Brothers and sisters who don't need as much attention — whether they're older or younger — often become jealous and angry. They might throw temper tantrums, which is a not-very-nice way of forcing the parents to pay attention!

This is called "sibling rivalry," because they feel they are competing for attention.

Of course, it's not your fault if you get more time with Mom and Dad than your brother or sister. You get what you NEED to get. It's no one's fault.

That's an important idea to remember, even if your brother or sister forgets. And it works the other way around, too. If you ever feel jealous that your sister or brother can do things you can't, it's OK to feel that. But do try to remember that it's not anybody's fault.

Angry feelings may come sometimes, but it's a little like being angry at the weather. Nobody's to blame.

Many disabilities are genetic, which means they are a trait that runs in your family. Even if your parents don't have your disability, they may have the genetic information inside them that carries it. And your brothers or sisters might have a form of your disability, too.

Of course, there can still be differences. Jenny's big sister Brittany has medical "problems," her mother says, which might be from a milder form of Jenny's disability.

Anna hangs with her twin brothers.

It's lucky for Jenny that Brittany doesn't need a lot of help, and that Brittany is old enough to understand why Jenny gets more of Mom's attention. "My sissy loves me, and she takes me riding in her truck when she's not with her boyfriend!" Jenny says.

Tips

Ask your parents if you can schedule special time with them without your brother or sister — and you might suggest they offer the same kind of one-on-one time with your sibling, too. A personalized shopping trip, or a private game played together, can go a long way to helping everybody feel loved.

Is there something you'd like to do with your brother or sister? Try asking. You might find that having your own just-us-kids activity helps your understanding of each other and creates a new kind of loving relationship. If you can't agree, offer to do something he or she wants if he or she will do something you want.

Sometimes your brother or sister may want to help you do something, but maybe he or she doesn't know what or how to ask. It may be up to you to find out or make suggestions.

Remember, don't be afraid to express your feelings.

Family Caregiving

"I like to be as independent as possible," says 11-year-old Anna. If you get at a lot of physical help from your parents, you know how tough it can be — on both of you. You need the help, but you don't like giving up your independence and privacy.

A big word that means the same thing is AUTONOMY. Say it like AW-TAH-NUM-MEE. Everybody likes to have autonomy. It doesn't mean you can do everything by yourself. It means you keep control over your care, have choices about what's done to and with your

"Parents shouldn't underestimate their children's possibilities."

— Anna Lennartson

life and your body, and take responsibility for whatever happens.

Kids don't have a lot of autonomy. But all parents want their kids to grow into happy, nice grownups who do have autonomy. And sometimes that takes practice.

"Parents shouldn't underestimate their children's possibilities," Anna says. "Let them be as independent as their disability lets them. In my opinion, no kid wants to be treated like a little 2-year-old just because of his or her disability. Kids with disabilities want to be treated like anyone else."

Talking About Change

When the time comes to find someone else to help with your personal care, it can be hard telling your parents. Sometimes you don't even know yourself that you want to do things a different way. Try asking yourself once a month: "Is there anything I want to change about the way my disability is handled?" Then talk about it with your parents.

Change can be a lot of fun. Anna's mother tells a story about when Anna got her first power wheelchair at age 6. "Instead of sitting on the sidelines watching the neighborhood kids ride their bikes and scooters, she was suddenly out there zooming around with them. Anna's wheelchair really gives her a lot of independence."

That's the key — independence. Imagine the independence other changes could bring. "We're looking into getting me a helper dog," says Anna, "especially for when I'm grown up and living on my own." (For more on helper dogs, see Chapter 4.)

Thinking about other times when a change turned out to be a good thing should help you feel better about a new change.

Sound scary? Yes, but remember that change is a part of growing up.

Making the Change

Hiring your first personal-care assistant (some people like the word "attendant" better) can be wonderful and scary.

"My parents have always helped me, but recently a girl who's a youth worker at our church moved in with us and now she helps me sometimes," says Amy, 14, who has cerebral palsy. "Suddenly I have a social life as people realize they can invite me places and I no longer come with a parent."

Amy felt nervous at first. She says she had to "learn to be independent." She learned to tell someone else how to do the things she needs. "I never needed a watch, because someone is always with me to keep track of time. Since I can't handle money with my fingers, others have always used it for me," Amy says. "Now I'm wondering if I can go to college since

I've never worn a watch or held money!"

Amy feels she still doesn't have "enough control. People try innovative things constantly without checking with me to see if I even like the new plan." But Amy has hope.

"I hope to still have a state-funded attendant when I get to college, so I won't have to bring my mother along!" she says. "This will determine whether the rest of my career goals will fly. I can't carry them out without college and an attendant, and I'd hate to bring my mother to college."

Tips

If you need help figuring out how to move from a family caregiver to someone new, remember that many other people have gone through the exact same thing.

About 30 years ago, people like you began what is called the "independent living movement." For more information, try:

1. The National Council on Independent Living: www.ncil.org

2. Dimenet: www.dimenet.com

3. The Virtual Independent Living Center: www.virtualcil.net. This one includes a directory of real independent living centers across the country.

"Keep trying to succeed," says Amy. "Don't feel sorry for yourself or blame people for your frustrations, because that's just a time-waster and doesn't solve anything."

Amy really wants to do a lot and go far, and she hopes she can make people see that "a person with a disability isn't just someone they should pity. We have real lives too, and can learn a lot and make a difference."

Will I Have a Family of My Own?

Most kids dream about growing up and making their own family. But many kids with disabilities wonder if it's even possible to have children later in life.

It's a very real worry. Even your doctor may not know the answer. The whole idea of people with disabilities growing up and having their own kids is still pretty new to many doctors — even though people have been doing it for years.

"I haven't decided if I want to get married or anything like that," says 11-year-old Anna.

But Jenny knows — and already knows who! "I want to marry Cody," she says.

The Facts

Did you know that more than one in

Illustration by Doug Davis

10 American families with children have at least one parent who has a disability?

That statistic comes from Through the Looking Glass, an organization in Berkeley, California, which is trying to make life easier for families that have a mom or dad with a disability (see www.lookingglass.org).

Of course, whether you'll be able to get married and have children depends on many different things. Will you meet the person of your dreams? Will your disability change as you get older? Will medicine and technology make things easier?

After all, what seemed impossible five years ago is now common.

For girls who hope to be a mom someday, the big question is about pregnancy. Again, the answer is, "It depends."

If you have cerebral palsy, it probably affects your muscle control. That can make having babies dangerous — but not impossible. You might need surgery or medical treatments to reduce the risks.

If you have a spinal curvature known as scoliosis, you probably can get pregnant, but you might need to stay in bed or in a hospital for a long time before the baby comes.

Anna says she "might like to adopt a kid" when she grows up. That's another choice many people like.

By the way, Anna's brittle-bones disorder does not usually make it impossible to have babies.

Still, having babies is less common for women with disabilities than women in general. That could be changing, however. One study found that more women with spinal cord injuries — broken backs — are having babies than ever before. "Normal labor and delivery are possible, even routine," the study said, "and generally pose little or no added risk to the mother or baby."

The Mattlins

My Success Story

Let me tell you about me: I was born with a muscle weakness called spinal muscular atrophy, and I met my wife when my stepmother hired her as a "mother's helper" one summer. My wife likes to joke that we were living together in the same house before we even dated!

Now we have two daughters, Paula and Miranda. But we had to go to special doctors for five years before we could have babies. At times, we thought it would never happen! Now those sad years are just a memory.

In Berkeley, California, many parents with disabilities work at Through the Looking Glass. They love to share their stories to help others. They do not say it was easy to have babies. But whether it's by pregnancy or adoption, becoming a parent is something many, many people who grew up with a disability can do.

"Have courage and hope for the future," says Anna. "Don't let things get you down or stop you from doing what you want to do. Anything is possible!" 🐾

BEN MATTLIN is a writer in Los Angeles. He was born in New York City with a disability called spinal muscular atrophy. He never walked or stood, and today uses a power wheelchair and software that allows him to control a computer by voice. He lives with his wife and their two daughters.

Would you like to see a color MAGAZINE called

Kids on Wheels?

Visit us on the Web at
www.kidsonwheels.us
and let us know what you think!

How Ed Roberts Changed the World

An empty blue wheelchair sits in the Smithsonian Institution, the national museum of the United States. That wheelchair belonged to my friend Ed Roberts.

Some of Ed's other friends brought his wheelchair all the way across the United States, from California to Washington, D.C. They left the Smithsonian a note saying the wheelchair had been donated to the museum.

Smithsonian curators, the people who take care of the museum, at first didn't know what to do with Ed's wheelchair. Then they thought if this wheelchair meant so much to people, the museum needed to learn more about the history of people with disabilities. They needed to learn why some people called Ed "the father of the independent living movement."

Boy Meets Wheels

Ed Roberts was born on January 29, 1939. His mother thought he looked like a rat with dark hair. As a child, Ed ran everywhere. He did not sit still long enough to learn to read until the fifth grade.

When Ed was 14, in 1953, he was a star athlete at his school. One afternoon he played in a baseball game. After he got home, he didn't feel well.

The next morning Ed had a fever and sore spine. Ed went to the hospital,

where the doctors said he had polio, a virus that can cause paralysis or even death. There is a vaccine now, but in those days, lots of kids ended up with permanent disabilities.

Ed stayed in the hospital for two years. Now, he could move only two fingers on his left hand, and two toes on his left foot. The rest of his body remained paralyzed, and he needed an "iron lung." The iron lung, a machine as big as a small car, looked like a tunnel on wheels. When Ed was inside the tunnel, the iron lung would do the work of breathing that his own lungs could no longer do.

After Ed got over being sick from the virus, he had to learn how to do lots of things all over again, like dressing and eating.

After Ed got out of the hospital, his

famous wheelers

Today's Famous Wheelers

There are many important wheelers in the world — far more than we have room to include in this book. But here are a few high-profile wheelchair users worthy of the term "role model."

Stephen Hawking is a famous British scientist with ALS (Amyotrophic Lateral Sclerosis). He is known for his brilliant work in understanding the physics of the universe. He wrote the bestselling books *A Brief History of Time and The Universe in a Nutshell*. To learn more, see his Web site: www.hawking.org.uk

Judith Heumann is a famous advocate for people with disabilities. A polio survivor, she encountered prejudice early in life and was at the front lines of the independent living movement. She held the highest appointed position of any wheelchair user in the federal government when she directed the Office of Special Education and Rehabilitation Services.

Christopher Reeve is a famous movie actor who played Superman on the big screen. After he was injured in a horseback riding accident, he used his fame to start the Christopher Reeve Paralysis Foundation, which funds cure research and other disability programs. To learn more, see the foundation's Web site: www.crpf.org

Marilyn Hamilton is a famous businesswoman who was one of the founders of the Quickie wheelchair company. Quickie is now owned by Sunrise Medical, and Marilyn has gone on to other projects, such as creating Winners on Wheels, a scouting organization for young wheelchair users (www.wowusa.com).

family moved into a different home because their old house didn't have room for Ed's iron lung and other equipment. In the new house the large dining room became Ed's bedroom.

No one else in Ed's school had polio. At first he participated in his classes with a phone hook-up. When Ed pushed a bar on the phone he could be heard, and when he let go of the bar he could hear.

Once a semester Ed's high school class met at his house. During Ed's senior year his mother, Zona, told him he had to attend classes once a week at the high school. Ed was scared stiff; he had not been to school since the eighth grade.

His greatest fear was that he would be stared at. He was. He finally decided that if people were always going to stare at him, he would work to be a star.

The Rolling Quads

After Ed graduated from high school, he went to a community college. He wore a big back brace to sit up for as long as could while going to classes.

Ed took a lot of time getting around campus and doing homework. He needed three years to finish two years of classwork. While he studied, Ed thought about what he wanted to do with his life. He decided he wanted to learn how government worked.

He learned that the University of California at Berkeley had a good program in government. Ed applied to go there.

Ed also asked the California Department of Rehabilitation for financial aid. The Department helped people with disabilities get training or education so they could work one day. But an employee there told Ed that he was too badly "crippled" to work. Ed and his friends fought this decision and won. Ed got some money.

Ed visited the Berkeley campus before the school year began. The people he met at the university were scared when they met Ed. They thought Ed might cause problems. No one knew where Ed would live. None of the dormitory rooms on campus, where many students lived, were big enough for his iron lung.

A doctor who worked at Cowell Hospital, the student health center, saw lots of people who'd had polio. He thought they should be able to go to college. He suggested Ed live at Cowell. Lots of people helped figure out ways Ed could do this.

When Ed went to Berkeley in 1962, he was the only student with a disability living at Cowell. As far as we know, he was also the first student with his level of disability to go to an American university.

A newspaper ran a story about Ed with the headline, "Helpless Cripple Goes to School." A social worker in a nearby town read the story. He worked with a student named John Hessler, whose neck had been broken in a diving accident. John also used a wheelchair, but he lived in a nursing home — that was more common for young quadriplegics in those days. (Most people didn't think wheelchair users could go to college, work and live independently.) John's social worker put John in touch with the university at Berkeley, and he soon joined Ed at Cowell. More students joined Ed and John in the following years. The University now had enough students with disabilities to begin a program planned to meet their needs.

Students living in Cowell Hospital had their own rooms. The hospital had a big room where they got together to talk or watch TV. They ate with each other in a dining room. They spent a lot of time together. They even gave themselves a name, the Rolling Quads. The time they spent together became important because they talked with each other about their lives, their hopes, and their goals and how to achieve them.

Chuck Close is a famous painter with quadriplegia. Museums and galleries all over the world have exhibited his artwork, which can also be found in several art books. Because he has limited hand movement, he has adapted his technique to create beautiful paintings on a very large scale. You can see some of his paintings at www.paceprints.com.

Harriet McBryde Johnson is a famous lawyer and writer with muscular dystrophy. She has served as chair of the Charleston Democratic Party, and in 2003 she wrote a cover story for *The New York Times Magazine* that landed her a book contract. In January 2004, she was named Person of the Year by *New Mobility* magazine, a wheelchair lifestyle magazine for adults.

John Hockenberry is a famous journalist who is paraplegic. He now works for Dateline NBC, and he has traveled all over the world covering stories for different news outlets, such as National Public Radio and ABC News. He is also known for his popular book, *Moving Violations: War Zones, Wheelchairs and Declarations of Independence*, his memoir of life as a foreign correspondent.

Ellen Stohl is a famous spokesperson for people with disabilities. As a teacher, she has the chance to educate a lot of people about spinal cord injuries (like hers) and other disabilities. She has also modeled for magazines to show that women who use wheelchairs are as beautiful as anyone. She is currently working on a documentary video about becoming pregnant and having a baby.

famous wheelers

Teddy Pendergrass is a famous singer known for his romantic "Teddy Bear" image. He was also the first black artist to record five consecutive platinum albums (meaning each one sold more than a million copies). After he was injured in a car accident in 1982, he stopped touring for a while. But he's back on stage now, singing from his wheelchair with the same flare that made him famous.

Jean Driscoll is a famous athlete with spina bifida who won the women's wheelchair division of the Boston Marathon eight times — more than any other athlete wheeling or running. She also holds two Olympic Silver medals, five Paralympic Golds (plus a handful of Silver and Bronze), and was named one of *Sports Illustrated*'s top 25 female athletes of the 20th century.

James Langevin is a famous politician with quadriplegia. As a representative for Rhode Island in the U.S. House of Representatives, he is currently the highest elected official who uses a wheelchair. (But remember — there has been a senator and even a president!) To learn more, see Congressman Langevin's Web site: www.house.gov/langevin

Dreaming Big

After Ed graduated, he learned about money that might be used to help other students. Ed talked John Hessler and others into asking for this money. They got it and started a program called the Physically Disabled Students Program (PDSP). They helped students with disabilities to succeed in college like they had.

Lots of people with disabilities from the San Francisco area wanted help from PDSP. Some of them weren't even students, but there was nowhere else they could go. They needed a program like PDSP.

So three of the Rolling Quads started planning a similar organization for the whole community: the Center for Independent Living (CIL). People who worked at CIL believed that people with disabilities were like everyone else except for their disabilities. They knew more about what it was like to live with a disability than anyone else. They were the experts about their own lives.

CIL started peer support programs. Someone with a disability helped others with disabilities learn how to get around the city in their wheelchairs, how to handle money, how to find an apartment, how to get a new wheelchair, how to act around people with other disabilities, and how to do many other tasks.

Ed ran CIL and made it famous first in the San Francisco area, then in California, then the United States, then all over the world. People from all over the United States and the world visited. Many people believe CIL is the place where the disability rights movement began.

Ed became known to lots of people. When Jerry Brown became governor of California in 1974, three of Brown's law school classmates were also Ed's friends. They suggested Ed become Director of the Department of Rehabilitation (DR). Brown met with Ed and appointed him DR Director. Now Ed was the boss of the DR employee who had told him he was "too crippled" to work!

About a year after that, Ed married Catherine McDugan. Ed and Cathy gave birth to their son, Lee Roberts, in 1978. The birth took place at home so Ed could help.

The marriage lasted only a few years; then Ed and Cathy had joint custody of

Lee. Ed brought Lee with him on his travels from an early age. Toward the end of his life, when people from all over the world asked Ed what he liked to be called, he usually replied, "Dad."

Ed had to leave his job at DR when Jerry Brown's time as governor ended. With two of his friends, Ed started planning an important new organization: the World Institute on Disability (WID).

Within a year, Ed got a call from the MacArthur Foundation. They asked if he would accept what is known as a "Genius" Fellowship. It's a five-year award to let people of great dreams follow their ideas without money worries. Part of the money goes to a program that the "genius" chooses. Ed used it to help WID.

Twenty years later WID is known all over the world for its projects.

Ed stayed at WID for the rest of his life. He traveled all over the world talking about disability rights.

A Lasting Legacy

On a March morning in 1995, Ed passed on. Thousands of people from all over the world attended a memorial service.

Lots of articles talked about Ed's life and importance. When Ed started going to college, he made it possible for thousands — maybe millions — of people with disabilities to do the same thing.

In 1974, the government of the United States said that children with disabilities of all ages could go to schools with children who didn't have disabilities.

The Physically Disabled Student's Program was the first program of its kind. Now almost every university and community college has a similar program.

The Center for Independent Living was the first organization of its kind. There are now more than 300 independent living centers in the United States and many more across the world.

Ed became the first person with his kind of disability to lead a state Vocational Rehabilitation agency. Many more have followed in his path.

The World Institute on Disability has grown from its beginnings of three people in 1983 to an organization of about 30 workers known throughout the world for many activities.

Other disability rights activists have received the MacArthur Genius Fellowship since Ed.

All of these are great accomplishments, but Ed's legacy may live on most in the individuals he met. At a memorial service held at WID shortly after Ed's death, a woman told the story of how her parents had moved to the United States from another country after she became disabled. She was in a hospital in the San Francisco area. She didn't know what to do with herself.

When her family asked if she wanted anything, she said she'd like to meet Ed. He came to see her. While he sat by her bed, she told Ed her story, and he began to cry. When she saw the tears that he could not wipe from his face, she knew that she could do things Ed could not do. Yet he was an influential, happy man in his huge, power wheelchair, breathing with the aid of a ventilator. She wondered why she was lying in a hospital bed. She got up and has since become a well-known artist in the Bay Area.

Many people before Ed helped make life better for people with disabilities. Since Ed died, lots of people have been doing the same thing. But Ed had an impact on so many people that he is a good choice to single out as one person with a disability who changed the world. 🏃

STEVEN E. BROWN is cofounder of the Institute on Disability Culture. A widely published author, he lives in Hawaii and travels all over the world to speak on disability issues.

A President on Wheels

One of the greatest presidents of the United States was a wheelchair user. Thing is, nobody knew it!

Franklin Delano Roosevelt, often called FDR, was paralyzed by polio in 1921. But he lived in a time when showing his disability was risky in politics — a lot of people thought disability meant weakness. So when he was elected president in 1932, he convinced the public that he could walk. The truth is, he had to lean on a podium to give speeches, and he was braced by people on both sides when he walked anywhere. He never "walked" very far because he was paraplegic!

He was such a popular president that newspaper reporters and photographers helped him keep his secret. He served four terms, but they never photographed him in his wheelchair or looking disabled in any way. The photo shown here is one of two known pictures showing our president on wheels.

The other photo shows the FDR Memorial in Washington, D.C. When the memorial was first planned, all of the exhibits showed the president standing, but disability advocates protested. They wanted the truth to be known: FDR was a strong leader who led the country through the Great Depression and World War II — *and* he used a wheelchair. At the time, Jim Dickson of the National Organization on Disability said, "We need this statue to tell all the children with disabilities and all their parents that anything is possible." The advocates got their way, and now people from all over the world visit the memorial and see the real FDR, our only president on wheels (so far!).

"The only thing we have to fear is fear itself."
— Franklin Delano Roosevelt

Julian Hirsmuller-Counts hangs out with FDR.

Photo by Gary Counts

Are you the next Famous Wheeler?

Tell Your Story!

Go to kidsonwheels.us and tell us why you (or someone you know) is an up-and-coming kid on wheels.

The first 20 writers will get a free gift!

www.kidsonwheels.us

KIDS ON WHEELS

your rights

By Jean Dobbs

Know the Law — It's Important!

S heri Koors was like a lot of young girls: She wanted to shop for jewelry and hair accessories at her local Claire's, one of 2,200 stores in the company's national chain. Since she was 6 years old, Sheri, who has spina bifida, struggled to get around in the crowded store. She tried not to knock over the displays, and she stretched her neck to try to use the high mirrors.

But soon after being crowned Miss Junior Wheelchair Florida, Sheri decided it was time to assert her rights under the Americans with Disabilities Act. With the help of Access Now, she filed a lawsuit against Claire's to force the stores to make room for kids on wheels.

The company finally agreed to redesign its shops to be more accessible. This was great news to Sheri, who said, "I'll probably be shopping there for a long time."

This is a good example of how the law can affect your everyday life. For anyone with a disability, the Americans with Disabilities Act (ADA) is a *very* important law.

Before the ADA, businesses didn't have to have ramps or elevators or clear paths through their stores. Before the ADA, companies could fire a person who became disabled, even if he or she could still do the job with a small change in the work environment. Before the ADA,

some government programs — including kids' activities — were not accessible. Now they have to be.

The truth is, the ADA is the reason you can find a space to sit at the movies, join your friends at Chuck E. Cheese, or wheel around a public park.

Things were not always this way. The ADA wasn't passed until 1990, when it was signed into law by the first President Bush. Because it's pretty new, you are the first generation of kids to grow up with this law!

How Does It Work?

While there are still some barriers and some people with bad attitudes, America is probably the best place in the world to have a disability. The ADA guarantees your *civil rights*, which basi-

145

cally means you have the same rights and freedoms as all American citizens and you must be treated equally under the law. If you are not treated equally, it is called *discrimination*.

If someone does discriminate against you, you can file a complaint with the U.S. Department of Justice to help enforce the ADA. You can also file a private *lawsuit*. This is a formal legal process for making businesses or governments follow the law.

Most of the time, you don't need to file a lawsuit to improve access. It is always best to try other ways first, like just talking to someone in charge. For example, your family's favorite restaurant might have a step at the only door. If you and your parents talk to the manager and explain that the law requires an accessible entrance, the restaurant may fix the problem to avoid a lawsuit (and to keep you as a customer).

One of the great things about know-

ing your legal rights is that you know you are not asking for "special" treatment. You are simply asking that people respect your right to do what everyone else does. And when people respect you, they can't pity you!

Alphabet Soup

There are a few terms in the ADA that may be confusing at first. Sometimes people will say that getting rid of a barrier is "readily achievable." This just means it is pretty easy to do and doesn't cost much money. Ramps are often a "readily achievable" way to remove a barrier like a step.

A similar term is "reasonable accommodation." This just means making a change that solves a problem and doesn't cause problems for other people. Moving a class from an inaccessible room to an accessible room nearby is a "reasonable accommodation." Or if an employee asks her company to raise her desk a few inches, that is a "reasonable accommodation."

Sometimes businesses will say that making a change would cause them "undue hardship." This usually means it would cost too much money or it would harm their business in some way. Sometimes this is true, and sometimes it is just an excuse to break the law.

It is worth taking the time to understand your legal rights as a person with a disability. There is a ton of information about the ADA on the official ADA Web site (www.ada.gov). You can also read about other laws, such as IDEA (the Individuals with Disabilities Education Act), which guarantees your right to equal education. And then there are laws that cover things like flying on airplanes and fair housing. Although the ADA is the biggest of the disability laws, they all work together to give you access to the same opportunities as all Americans.

The ABCs of the ADA

The ADA prohibits discrimination on the basis of disability. The law covers employment, state and local government, public places, businesses, transportation, and telecommunications. It also applies to the United States Congress.

A person with a disability is defined by the ADA as a person who has a physical or mental impairment that substantially limits one or more major life activities (like walking).

Title 1: Employment

Title 1 says employers with 15 or more employees can't discriminate against people with disabilities. They must provide "reasonable accommodation" unless it would cause "undue hardship."

Title 2: State and Local Government

This part of Title 2 says that state and local government programs must be accessible to people with disabilities. This includes both services and physical locations. (Usually this means buildings, but it might also include something like adding a curb cut to a sidewalk.)

Title 2: Public Transportation

This part of Title 2 says public transportation (like buses and trains) should be accessible. When this is not possible, there must be *paratransit*. Paratransit is a service that picks up and drops off people with disabilities.

Title 3: Public Accommodations

Title 3 says that businesses and organizations open to the public (like restaurants or movie theaters) must treat people with disabilities as they would anyone else. Buildings and services must be made accessible if it is "readily achievable." This might be something as simple as adding a grab bar to a bathroom.

Stricter rules about access must be followed when a business remodels or builds something new. The rules get pretty specific about how wide doorways should be and how steep ramps can be. You should be able to safely use a ramp by yourself (without someone pushing you or waiting to catch you!)

One of the interesting things in this section of the law is about service animals. Service animals (like seeing eye dogs or other service dogs), must be allowed into public places even if those places don't usually allow animals.

Title 4: Telecommunications

Title 4 deals with telephone and television access for people with hearing and speech disabilities. For example, it says that phone companies need to have a way for callers with hearing and speech disabilities to use the phone.

Title 5: Miscellaneous

Title 5 deals with some details that keep the law working the way it should.

• For more information about the ADA, contact the ADA Information Line at 800-514-0301 (Voice) or 800-514-0383 (TDD). Also check out the Web site at www.ada.gov. If you still can't find what you need, contact the U.S. Department of Justice, Civil Rights Division, 950 Pennsylvania Ave., NW, Disability Rights Section, Washington, D.C. 20530.

Think you get it?

Try the ADA crossword puzzle on the next page. If you get stumped, you can always go back and reread a section — all of the answers are in this chapter. For the key to the puzzle, look on page 150, but try not to peek until you finish!

ADA Crossword

14. Businesses may say that a change to improve access would cause "undue hardship." This means it would _____ their business.

16. The Americans with Disabilities Act grants civil rights to people with disabilities. One result is that people are more often seen as equals, not objects of ____.

17. The Americans with Disabilities Act and the Individuals with Disabilities Education Act are examples of these.

18. Something a company might do to an employee with a disability instead of providing a "reasonable accommodation."

ACROSS

1. Something that makes a place inaccessible.

5. The Department of _____ enforces the Americans with Disabilities Act.

7. The Title of the Americans with Disabilities Act that applies to state and local governments.

8. Something you might do if a public restroom didn't have a grab bar.

9. The president who signed the Americans with Disabilities Act into law.

10. If it's accessible, it has a cut.

12. Seeing ____ dogs are one type of service animal that must be allowed in public places under the Americans

with Disabilities Act.

DOWN

2. What the Americans with Disabilities Act says we should do to barriers.

3. Places covered under Title 3 of the Americans with Disabilities Act.

4. A common barrier.

6. The purpose of the Americans with Disabilities Act.

7. The Title of the Americans with Disabilities Act that covers movie theaters.

11. One of the most "readily achievable" ways to make a place accessible.

13. 1990 is the _____ the Americans with Disabilities Act was signed into law.

15. The abbreviation for the Americans with Disabilities Act.

About the Editor

JEAN DOBBS has been writing about "life on wheels" for 13 years. She currently works from her home in Santa Monica, California, as editorial director of NEW MOBILITY, a color lifestyle magazine for adult wheelchair users. The magazine grew out of a resource guide called SPINAL NETWORK: THE TOTAL WHEELCHAIR RESOURCE BOOK, which Jean now publishes.

If you would like to see a color magazine grow out of KIDS ON WHEELS, write to Jean at P.O. Box 1767, Santa Monica, CA 90406. You can also e-mail her at jean@kidsonwheels.us. Tell her what you'd like to read about in a magazine!

ADA Crossword Answer Key

					¹B	A	R	R	I	E	R	²R	
	³P		⁴S									E	
⁵J	U	S	T	I	C	E	⁶E					M	
	B		E				Q		⁷T	W	O	
⁸S	L	I	P		⁹B	U	S	H			V	
	I					A		R			E	
	¹⁰C	U	¹¹R	B		L		E				
		A			I		¹²E	¹³Y	E	
¹⁴H	¹⁵A	R	M			T			E	
	D		¹⁶P	I	T	Y			A	
¹⁷L	A	W	S				¹⁸F	I	R	E

150